—DONALD E. WILDMON
Chairman, American Family Association

"Eva Marie and Jessica Everson's book *Sex, Lies, and the Media* is a readable, much-needed overview of the cultural snares, trials, and temptations that our young people face. Written from the point of view of a concerned mother and her daughter, it is an important, eye-opening building block in the media-wise tools for parents with faith and values. We face a crisis in the mass media of entertainment's brainwashing of our children and grandchildren, and this book is the first step in extricating our children and grandchildren from the clutches of the mass media."
—DR. TED BAEHR
Chairman, Christian Film and Television Commission and Publisher, Movieguide

"This dynamic mother/daughter duo add an important voice to the national dialogue on sex and the media. Their thoughtful and well-thought-out words allow us all to take a deep breath on the subject and evaluate what course of action we wish to take. This book reminds us that we are all susceptible to believing false images and ideals. It challenges us to look inside, dig deeper, and never, never stop talking to our children about this issue."
—JESSICA WEINER
Author of *A Very Hungry Girl; How I Filled Up On Life And How You Can, Too*

"This book should be required reading for every parent of a teenager. Eva Marie and Jessica Everson have done a fabulous job of unveiling the damaging influences of the media. Parents are left without excuse—they have done the homework for us."
—VICKI COURTNEY
Founder of Virtuous Reality; National Speaker and Best-selling Author of *Your Girl: Raising a Godly Daughter in an Ungodly World*

"In this no-nonsense guide for parents, Eva Marie and Jessica Everson equip parents with the tools to understand the forces in our culture that negatively influence the next generation—and offer practical suggestions on how to deal with them. Well-researched and to-the-point, this book will be a handy reference for parents who want to understand the world of their kids."
—STEVEN JAMES
Popular conference speaker and author of the teen devotionals *How to Smell Like God* and *Praying From the Gut*

"This is a landmark book for parenting in the twenty-first century and represents a major contribution to moral excellence in rearing children to successful emancipation. My thinking was reordered as I read this manuscript, and I marked page after page of important safeguards necessary to raise pure kids in an impure world. Astonished, informed, encouraged, equipped...these are the buzzwords that will be swirling around this deeply vital book."
—RENEE DURFIELD, D.D.
Author of *Raising Pure Kids in an Impure World*
Executive Director, For Wedlock Only   OCT 0 1 2005

"Eva Marie and Jessica Everson address the much needed topic of how to navigate the waters of media and popular culture. The findings of this well-researched book may well shock some Christians who've had their heads comfortably buried in the sand. Our kids—not just 'those other' kids, but even Christian kids—are not only surrounded by, but are also imitating, the sexual permissiveness that they're watching in films and TV and hearing in their music. So what's a parent to do? The Eversons first open our eyes, then offer some practical helps. As an actress myself for the past twenty years, I especially appreciated their point of view: they didn't simply condemn media as a whole, nor do they ignore the reality of its presence and impact on our lives. Instead, with biblical insights and practical suggestions, they re-empower parents to be parents. And part of that responsibility is to teach children to become wise consumers of the media they watch and the music they listen to. This is a book that every family needs to read."
—NANCY STAFFORD
Actress (*Matlock*), speaker, and author of *The Wonder of His Love: A Journey into the Heart of God* and *Beauty by the Book: Seeing Yourself as God Sees You*

"A 'no apologies' and 'in-your-face' Christian response to the in-your-face affront of the secular media in the lives of our children. Eva Marie and Jessica Everson tell it like it is so we as parents can tell it like it is to our kids."
—VICKI CARUANA
America's Teacher™, author of the best-selling book *Apples and Chalkdust* and *Giving Your Child the Excellence Edge.*

"Years ago as a teen mom, I made devastating choices that changed the course of my life. I bought into the worldly lies of sex, drugs, and rock-n-roll, filling the empty places in my heart and soul with even emptier promises and pursuits. My life changed when I made my U-turn toward God. Eva Marie and Jessica Everson tell it like it is in this powerful and eye-opening must-read, giving today's parents and teens a chance to make life-changing U-turns of their own—based on truth."
—ALLISON BOTTKE
Author/Speaker, God Allows U-Turns

"Eva Marie and Jessica Everson's book gives discouraging facts with positive suggestions. I believe this book will be valuable resource for both parents and youth workers."
—JAMES LI (JAMES SANG LEE)
Youth Ministries Director, Northland: A Church Distributed
Martial Arts Champion and Movie Stuntman

"For parents crying for help against the intrusion of media, *Sex, Lies, and the Media* answers their pleas. For parents who aren't aware of the snares of media, *Sex, Lies, and the Media* opens their eyes. This "nothing-held-back" look at today's world, arms all parents with the weaponry needed to win the battle for the souls of their children."
—JILL RIGBY
Author of *Raising Respectful Children in a Disrespectful World*
President and CEO of Manners of the Heart Community Fund

SEX, LIES, AND THE MEDIA

EVA MARIE EVERSON
JESSICA EVERSON

 LIFE JOURNEY®

Bringing Home the Message for Life

COOK COMMUNICATIONS MINISTRIES
Colorado Springs, Colorado • Paris, Ontario
KINGSWAY COMMUNICATIONS LTD
Eastbourne, England

Life Journey® is an imprint of
Cook Communications Ministries, Colorado Springs, CO 80918
Cook Communications, Paris, Ontario
Kingsway Communications, Eastbourne, England

SEX, LIES, AND THE MEDIA
© 2005 by Eva Marie Everson and Jessica Everson

Published in association with the literary agency of The Knight Agency,
577 South Main St., Madison, GA 30650.

Cover Design: BMB Design/Scott Johnson

First Printing, 2005
Printed in the United States of America
Printing/Year
10 9 8 7 6 5 4 3 2 1   10 09 08 07 06 05

Unless otherwise noted, Scripture quotations are taken from the HOLY
BIBLE: NEW INTERNATIONAL VERSION®. Copyright © 1973, 1978,
1984 by International Bible Society. Used by permission of Zondervan. All
rights reserved. Scripture quotations marked NASB are taken from the
New American Standard Bible®. Copyright © 1960, 1962, 1963, 1968,
1971, 1972, 1973, 1975, 1977, 1995 by The Lockman Foundation. Used by
permission. Italics in Scripture have been added by the authors for
emphasis.

The Web site addresses (URLs) recommended throughout this book are
solely offered as a resource to the reader. The citation of these Web sites
does not in any way imply an endorsement on the part of the authors or
the publisher, nor do the authors or publisher vouch for their content for
the life of this book.

ISBN 0781441951

To Jordynn, Jordan, Savannah, and Baby Bynum.
You are the next generation of my heart.
My prayers are daily for you.
And to Ken "Bop" and Susan Wales. You inspire me.

—EME

To Jared A. Marchman (1983–2003).
Your friendship will never fade from my heart.
To God for making me just who he made me.
And to all those who helped me to become
the person I am today.

—JE

Contents

Foreword

Oh, I wish I could be a kid again!
Not because I suffer from the Peter Pan Syndrome of not wanting to grow up. To the contrary, in my fifty-second year, I'm enjoying my life, my wife of almost thirty years, and my two grown children, Jacob and Christy.

Having raised these two bright children into young adults, I know from experience that parenting is the toughest job on earth. That's a generational truth. The beauty of family life is that we get to pass on our values to the next generation. But the dark side is that the sexual brokenness that occurs in one life can negatively affect others for generations.

But, thanks in large part to the media, it's harder today to pass on our values than it has ever been. There is simply no escaping the sexualized messages of the culture, and the consequences are more serious than most parents imagine.

And so I wish I could be a kid again. If I could, I would take my kids back with me and show them what life was like when I was a youngster. A time when my friends and I could take bike hikes in the summer for five or six hours, and Mom had no need to worry about us being abducted or approached by unscrupulous strangers. A time when we spent countless hours playing pickup baseball in the street after dinner with the neighbor kids, and the only caution needed was moving second base due to the periodic interruption of cars coming down the street.

The adolescent years of every child should be built on an endless list of experiences that support wholeness and strength in their character as they mature. Ideally, as they look back on those years, they will be filled with fond memories. And innocence.

But the harsh reality for children today—and the children of all the todays after today—is that we are now living in a culture where lyricists, entertainment executives from Hollywood to New York City, marketers and advertisers of products ranging from clothing to soft drinks, and shock-jocks heard on radio stations from every community across our land are all helping exploit a single reality in their messages: SEX SELLS.

The sex-saturated environment we live in and the brokenness it produces due to the one-dimensional message of sex will continue to impact not only our children's generation but also countless generations to come. We cannot escape it. Music defines it. Television demands it. "Family viewing hour" is no longer a safe choice. Walking through a shopping mall with kids in tow represents a different set of challenges for parents. Young children have the opportunity to see larger-than-life-size posters of naked models, displayed for the purpose of advertising clothing and cologne, and parents are forced to explain why the model in the display window isn't dressed the way young ladies with modesty dress.

Even a trip to a local convenience store becomes a challenge as a parent attempts to shield the innocent eyes of his or her children from magazine covers.

The harsh reality for parents is that our children are being influenced—strongly influenced—not by our values, but by an entity that exploits healthy adolescent interest in the opposite sex.

Each month, as the National Coalition for the Protection of

Children and Families' senior vice president for strategic partnerships and Internet safety, I travel around this nation speaking to teens, parents, educators, and faith leaders, and I have learned a few things about what kids really want and need from their parents. First, moms and dads, you must *learn to listen* to your kids and then *listen to learn* what they have just told you. It is never too early or too late to begin listening to your children about the traps and snares they face as they travel through their adolescent years.

Second, you must assume the mantle of God-given authority for raising your children as wise King Solomon wrote in Proverbs 22:6. Educators and faith leaders alike share frequently with me, telling me of parents who drag their kids to youth group and Sunday school in hopes that youth leaders and teachers will "set them straight" on matters of sex. But, parents, this is your responsibility. The church's is to enforce the values youngsters are being taught at home.

So what are parents supposed to do? How is it possible for them to know all the ins and outs of media and its influence on their children? How can they fight a battle that often seems bigger than all our efforts combined?

Well, if you've picked up this book, you're at a very good starting point. The collaborative efforts of mother-and-daughter team Eva Marie and Jessica Everson have resulted in an honestly written, easy-to-read handbook for parents that will help you to understand the range of issues faced by your children.

As a young woman barely into her twenties, Jessica gives excellent insights into the power that media have on kids. Her unique perspective will not only capture your attention but also motivate you to have that talk you may have been putting off.

Eva Marie's ability to tell a dramatic story through the written word brings great power to the subject matter. Having spent hours upon hours in research, she writes in a "hold nothing back" fashion that will put you one step ahead of media moguls.

Together, they remind us that as bad as we perceive the culture is today, these are our children's "good old days," and the responsibility for making them the best of years rests with you.

You alone must take it. Starting here. Starting now.

—Jack L. Samad
Senior Vice President for Strategic Partnerships and Internet Safety
National Coalition for the Protection of Children and Families

Introduction

"What's a Nice Girl Like Me Doing in a Place Like This?"

Have nothing to do with the fruitless deeds of darkness, but
rather expose them.

—EPHESIANS 5:11

I am consumed by pornography.

It's true. Every day I am surrounded by the very issues that
Jesus instructed us to avoid.

Allow me to explain. As a published author and columnist, I
sit at a computer nearly all day. Due to the amount of research
that must be done for my work, I pretty much stay online. I have
four email addresses and one Web site. I answer approximately
fifty emails on any given day. I send out nearly twice as many.
My buddy list has nearly a hundred names of writer friends,
brothers and sisters in the Lord, and even those I pray will one
day join me in this journey of faith. Periodically I send or receive
an instant message (IM) to or from one of them—sometimes just
a hello.

Sometimes work that must be discussed or a prayer request
that needs lifting up comes my way via the little box in the upper
left-hand corner. In between all this computer conversation, I
search the Web and check my email, deleting those messages

that offend my sensibilities. I deleted unwanted IMs at least four or five times an hour. I barely even read them, but from what I can tell, a girl named Julie ... or is it Bambi ... or Ashley ... or some such name, who is eighteen years old, has just had her photos taken and wants me to take a look at them. Naturally she is naughty and naked and just purring for some fun. I'm not interested, so I click the X, though I have been known to send back a "Jesus loves you" message.

Not that I really think it will matter much to the man sitting on the other side of the screen, but you never know.

Back in 1997 I began writing what would become a fiction trilogy. *Shadow of Dreams, Summon the Shadows,* and *Shadows of Light*[1] tell the story of a redeemed exotic dancer. I couldn't have known it then, but God was about to open up a whole new world to me—one in which I'd only dabbled in my earlier years. For example, there was the time my friend and I discovered a *Playboy* magazine in her teenage brother's bathroom and stole a look at it. Or the time my brother and I found the peek-aboo calendar my great-uncle had hidden behind a dresser in the musty, shut-off spare bedroom located in the far corner of the Victorian he shared with my great-aunt. What should have struck me then (but only strikes me now) is that pictures of naked women were always hidden, and that, whether with my friend or my brother, I was always doing my best to avoid getting caught looking at them.

In 2002, when the second book of the trilogy was released, a reporter from the Billy Graham Evangelistic Association's *Decision Today* radio broadcast interviewed me. During that interview I spoke of the necessity of the church—as well as individuals—getting involved in reaching out to those who are in the sex-for-sale industry. One listener was a woman named Sue who worked for the National Coalition for the Protection of Children and Families (NCPCF), which began as the National Coalition

Against Pornography (NCAP). Shortly after that interview, I received an email from Sue informing me of the work of the Coalition and suggesting ways we might be able to serve one another in our ministries.

Now I have to be honest. My first thought was "What exactly is my ministry here? I mean, other than writing fiction?"

Oh, sure. In addition to writing my world of make-believe, I could easily talk about what the church and individuals need to do or should do, but that pretty much summed up what I thought of as my participation: I told others what they needed to do, and then they did it. It had always worked for me.

But I emailed something back to Sue like, "Well, sure, let me see what you've got."

And she did. She sent me an impressive package filled with pamphlets, brochures, and other booklets telling about the problems in our society as they relate to porn. I was both impressed and a little concerned.

In the meantime, I kept writing, working hard to get out that third book. This writing was, after all, my part in the war against porn. Then, one day as I was minding my own business, my phone rang. It was Sue from the Coalition, informing me that the vice president of the Coalition would be in my little corner of North America and would like to meet with me.

"Uh … sure," I said, a bit reluctantly. After all, he is a man, I am a woman, and we're going to be talking about *sex*. But Sue spoke so highly of this professional, I thought, "Well, why not?"

We set up a time and place to meet. As soon as I hung up the phone, I went back to my desk, where I logged on to the Web site of the Coalition, searching for some information about this man with whom I would soon be having breakfast at a restaurant off Interstate 4. An hour later, mission accomplished, I felt pretty good about the whole thing. The man looked nice enough from his photo, and I was fairly impressed with his work, titled

Sex and Young America.[2] But nothing could have prepared me for the one-hour—stretched to four-hour—meeting I would have with Jack Samad. What Jack showed me that morning inspired me to become more involved in the war against pornography and the effects it has on our young people.

"Jack," I said when our time was complete, "just let me get through writing this third novel. Then, I'm yours. I'll do anything I can to join in the fight."

Soon after the dawn of 2003, *Shadows of Light* was finished and the manuscript was in the hands of my trusty editor. Between the dreaming and the coming true, anytime I came across pertinent information about media, pornography, and our youth, or news on these subjects from the Internet, I placed it in a stack to the left side of my desk. By the time I got around to actually reading it, it was a bit imposing.

Studies show the average child spends only seventeen hours a week with his parents.

—Pamela Kruger in *Child* magazine[3]

At Jack's suggestion, I took a little trip to a nearby bookstore and purchased some "teen magazines." Back at home I sat in my favorite chair and began to rip out the pages I thought offensive for teenage girls. When I had finished, I had only shells of the magazines left to throw in the trash.

I went headfirst into Internet porn, especially porn aimed at or about children. I wrote complaints to companies that use soft-porn advertising on television. One vitamin company told me they were unaware their commercial was being aired during a time when children could be watching and promised to have it removed. To my knowledge, the company did as promised. I felt pretty good, knowing that my one voice had made a difference.

I joined OneMillionMoms.com. I began to take note of

videos, TV shows, movies, and so forth. I learned things I wished I did not know. While I was at a speaking engagement in Houston, Texas, a conferee slipped me a small piece of paper as I signed one of my books for her. She whispered, "I wrote down the name of an organization in Austin that helps girls come out of the exotic dance clubs."

I thanked her, slipped the note into my nearby purse, and upon returning home contacted the organization. The next thing I knew, I was doing all I could to help promote the Magdalene Project.[4]

One morning, as I prayed about my work and what appeared to be my new ministry, I asked God, "Do you want me walking into the clubs around here, Lord?"

A friend of mine, a pastor's wife, had done so. For four months in 1999, she made weekly trips to a nearby "gentleman's club." She went into the dressing rooms and just talked with the girls. She took them gifts. If they had children, she took the children gifts as well. Eventually, inspired by my friend's witness for the Lord, several of the women left the business.

Her story inspired me enough to work the fabric of it into my second novel.

But could I do what she had done? My friend is very spunky and daring, and, quite honestly, I am not.

As I was praying, God gave me a revelation. I saw two doors. One led into a dance club, but the one before it led into the now proverbial "average American home" with a father and mother, 2.5 children, and a few domesticated animals. "Here's the problem," I felt the Spirit whisper to me. "My people are perishing for lack of knowledge" (Hos. 4:6, paraphrased).

Just after this revelation, I was speaking to a youth pastor who told me of some "incidents" he'd had to deal with at a recent retreat for the church's youth group. "Parents think that just because they are Christians and their homes are deemed as

The whole plan of attack is to desensitize this generation. The line is not a fixed line. It's movable. Every time someone challenges that line, it moves a bit, so what would have shocked us even six months ago, no longer does. What is shocking us today won't bother us in even less than a year. If the devil can erode a generation enough to say sex outside of marriage is okay, then pretty soon everything's okay. The problem with the church is they have no clue as to what's going on. No concept. It blows me away the issues they choose to make a stand on and the issues they choose to ignore.

—Chris Russell[5]

Christian homes, their children are immune to what the world is shoving in their faces," he told me.

I began to notice the number of my church's youth who wore clothing with the logo of Abercrombie and Fitch—one of the top clothiers of America's young people. This company uses, of all things, nudity in its advertising. Their catalog, called a "mag-alog," is about sex. It is age restricted, and Web sites for local A and F stores come with this warning: "Beware: there are more shots of flesh than fashion."

I noted the number of Christian young girls and women wearing shorts and slacks with words written across the buttocks, cute little sayings like Princess, Available, Hottie, and even Back-Off. I wondered, "Why not just write, 'Calling all lustful men, sexual perverts, and assorted pedophiles: look at my tushy'?"

"Will these girls be offended," I also wondered, "when some guy makes what they perceive as an unwelcome pass?"

Even more shocking are the number of stories I've heard (and my Christian author and speaker friends have been told) about the sexual escapades that take place within "churched" youth. For example, in her book *Your Girl*[6] author Vicki Courtney tells the story of a slumber party gone mad. While middle-school girls had their party, a group of their male peers was checking out some Internet porn sites. Later, the boys called the girls, telling them in graphic sexual detail what they'd like to do to them.

Guess what. These kids were "churched."

My friend Jack Samad tells similar stories. "Young girls—as young as eleven and twelve—have learned that they can attend boys' sleepovers, strip, and let the boys take a peek, and earn a hundred dollars of the boys' allowance. It's popular, and it's happening across America."

Even with Christian youth? You bet. Anyone who researches church youth and sexuality knows about George Barna and his comprehensive research. According to his 2001 report, 83 percent of teens believe that moral truth depends on the circumstances, and only 6 percent believe that moral truth is absolute. When it comes to believing in absolute truth, only 9 percent of born-again teenagers believe in moral absolutes.[7]

I spoke to a group of mothers from a nearby church. During my one-hour presentation—in which I could barely begin to present this topic—I saw more mouths gaped open than closed. Several eyes filled with tears: an indication that the women, their husbands, or their children were either battling pornography's vicious claws or were grievously concerned for the future generations. A pastor's wife approached me after the meeting. "Can you come back?" she asked. "Can you speak to all the parents? We really need to hear what you have to say."

I told her I would.

"We just had no idea," she concluded.

"Yes," I thought. "I had no idea either."

What you will read in the following chapters comes from my research into the world of sex for sale. If you, as a Christian parent (or even a parent with no religious sympathies), think that the dark side of sex is only going on in the shadowy streets and red-light districts of your city, town, or community—think again. If you have a television, computer, CD or cassette tape player, VHS or DVD player, cell phones, or current books and magazines in your house, then pornography is in your home. It is breeding in front of your children. It beckons them to become a part of a lifestyle that is "their right as human beings."

Sex, Lies, and the Media is my first writing collaboration with my twenty-something-year-old daughter. When I first told Jessica about the project, going over every chapter and subchapter, she had such insight from a young person's perspective that I asked her to be a part of the project with me. When she agreed, I was both thrilled and a bit nervous; Jessica brings to this work an element of raw honesty and bold enlightenment. Her work is the part that may bother you the most because, as a young woman herself, she has her finger on the pulse of today's youth. She is also blessed to be both spiritually wise and street smart.

The first step to media wisdom is to put parents into the media mix.

—Dr. Ted Baehr, chairman of the Christian Film and Television Commission[8]

More than just the facts, this book will contain what God's Word says about sex and intimacy, offering scriptural alternatives and parental advice from experts, of which I am not one. I am, quite simply, a parent/novelist who took her head out of the sand(box) for a moment, forced her eyes open, and then learned the truth about sex, lies, and the media.

CHAPTER 1

"We Didn't Do Things Like That in My Day"

The History of Sex

Remember your Creator in the days of your youth, before the days of trouble come and the years approach when you will say, "I find no pleasure in them."

—ECCLESIASTES 12:1

have always been a fan of old Tarzan movies. When I was a little girl, they came on every Saturday morning at ten o'clock and on Sunday afternoons at two. My mother would rise early on Saturday, get the house in order, call my brother and me from our play, sit between us on the sofa, and together we would thrill to Johnny Weissmuller and Maureen O'Sullivan (or whomever else was playing Tarzan and Jane in a particular film) as they swung from tree to tree, rode elephants, called to one another in their trademark "Ahhhhhhhhh ... ah ... ah ... aaaah ... aha ..." yell, played with Cheetah (their pet chimpanzee) and Boy (their son), and brought the jungle to rights.

On Sundays it was important to hurry through "Sunday dinner" (which, in the South, means lunch) and get the dishes washed, dried, and put away so we could relax again in the family room for the next old black-and-white fantasy. Old Tarzan movies hold, for me, precious memories of sitting close to my mother, eating stove-popped popcorn, drinking Kool-Aid, and sharing a joy.

When I was in my thirties, I found myself one afternoon perusing a video store. When I came to the classics section, I noticed an entire row of old Tarzan black and whites lined up according to release. I grabbed *Tarzan the Ape Man* (1932) and its first sequel, *Tarzan and His Mate* (1934), then headed home to microwave some popcorn, pop the top on a soft drink, cuddle with a blanket on the sofa, and watch these old classics.

I phoned my mother between Movie #1 and Movie #2, telling her of my find, and how the movies had been digitally remastered, and how Johnny Weissmuller was still as much of a "hunk" in the 1990s as he was in the 1930s, and "Mother, I've got to go watch *Tarzan and His Mate* before my family gets home!"

I popped Movie #1 out of the VCR, inserted Movie #2, and then sat back to enjoy. Minutes later I paused the movie, ran back to the phone, called my mother again, and—upon her answer—exclaimed, "Did you know Jane swims completely nude for like three and a half minutes in this film?"

My mother declared that she did not remember that little fact.

"Well, she does. I didn't know filmmakers did things like that back then," I said, shaking my head.

My mother assured me that sex was not a new thing.

I went back to the film and was again aghast at the scene in which Jane's English visitors bring her some perfume (which she applies to her neck). Enter Tarzan. Tarzan sniffs Jane. Tarzan says, "Jane smell good."

Jane says, "It's called perfume."

Tarzan then scoops Jane over his shoulder and heads for the tree house.

Hmm.

I learned that day that sex and the media have been holding hands for a long time.

As I researched for my novels, I discovered that sex and history pretty much go hand in hand.

Consider This

In ancient Mesopotamia—in part modern-day Iraq and located in the Tigris and Euphrates Valley—the primary deity was the goddess Ishtar. Part of Ishtar's rule was that of sexual power—that and war. (Go figure.)

Because she was the goddess of all things sexual and of all things pertaining to war, when the fighting men experienced victory, her dedicated temple would celebrate with food and sex. During this period of history, when a woman married, she was to go to the temple and then sit until a stranger approached and threw a piece of silver in her lap. This action, in effect, purchased the woman for sexual purposes after which the woman could return home.

Not surprisingly within this time period are some of the first references to sexually transmitted diseases (now often referred to as STDs). Ancient Egyptians give us some interesting—if not disgusting—references to birth control, abortion, and incest. Animal dung was used as spermicide. Potions were used to induce miscarriages. Because the Egyptians traced their lineage, and property was handed down through women (which meant that when a woman died, her husband lost

To stay healthy, you've got two choices. 1) Don't have sex. Abstinence is the only foolproof way not to get pregnant or get an infection. 2) If you are sexually active, use a new condom (latex or polyurethane) or dental dam (a six-inch-square piece of thin latex placed over the woman's vagina to prevent getting or giving an STD during oral sex) every time you have any kind of sex. (Yeah, any kind: oral, anal, vaginal, magical, radical ... you get the idea.) Also, get regular checkups, and talk to your partner about both your sexual histories. If you do get an STD, it's not the end of the world. STDs have been around forever, and many are curable or at least treatable, so don't despair.

—MTV.com[1]

not only his wife but also his property), it was common for fathers and daughters, brothers and sisters to marry in order to keep material goods.

The Renaissance began in Italy during the 1300s. When it ended around 1600, it had spread to parts of northern Europe and had brought new attitudes within virtually every aspect of culture. In this time period, men kept traditional wives as well as numerous mistresses and enjoyed an almost gamelike pursuit of the wives of other men.

In the Victorian Age (1830–1901), women had "special friends" (i.e., lovers) who were also women.

In 1886, Richard Krafft-Ebling wrote and published *Psycophathica Sexualis*, a book discussing sexual oddities. In 1903 the first nude colony was established. Soon thereafter, Sigmund Freud stunned the world by linking adult sexuality to childhood memories.

The 1950s brought the Kinsey report, an extensive volume of work that explored human sexuality (and which recently spawned a Hollywood movie), and the very first printing of *Playboy* magazine.

The 1960s introduced "The Sexual Revolution" and, along with it, the catchphrase "Make Love, Not War."

So why am I telling you all this? Because, as the author of Ecclesiastes wrote, "There is nothing new under the sun" (1:9). If you think sexual immorality didn't exist a hundred years ago or two hundred years ago or even thousands of years ago, think again. Even the Bible tells its own sordid stories, most of them hidden from our eyes, thanks—in part—to translation changes. But let's face it, Abraham married his half-sister, Tamar slept with her father-in-law, the mother of Boaz was a prostitute, David committed adultery with Bathsheba, and the biblical town of Sodom is where we get the word *sodomy*.

The list goes on and on.

The Enemy—our enemy, Satan—has been using sex to separate God and man since sin's first appearance on earth. Yet he is cunning—and sneaky. He has taken his time, which is one of his greatest assets: patience. The changes in the last fifty to one hundred years—especially as they relate to modern media—have been so subtle that as a parent you may or may not have noticed them. Or you may not have noticed them entirely. The truth is, what, at one time, was being done outside the bonds of God's holy order for husband and wife is now being openly exposed to the innocent eyes of our children on a daily, hourly, even moment-to-moment basis.

So, parent, it's time to get educated. Sit back. Prepare yourself for the truth. The whole truth. The truth that your kids won't tell you.

Children have a way of driving you to your knees.

—Mary Webb[2]

STATISTICALLY SPEAKING

Let's begin by getting specific with statistics.

According to George Barna, in 1999, 82 percent of polled teens said they were Christian.[3]

Sounds pretty good, doesn't it?

Well, hold on. There's more—and it's not necessarily good news.

- More than 61 percent of all high school seniors have had sexual intercourse. (When asked about sexual activity, most teens admit they do not consider anything outside of intercourse, i.e., oral, anal, or digital, as "sex.") Nearly 50 percent of these seniors are currently sexually active. More than 21 percent have had four or more sexual partners.
- The United States has the highest teen pregnancy rate in the world.
- Our adolescents have the highest STD rates.

- More than 25 percent of all sexually active adolescents this year will contract an STD, which accounts for more than three million cases.
- Two-thirds of those who contract an STD are twenty-five years of age and under.[4]
- A recent study from the Minnesota Department of Public Health found that out of thirteen hundred adolescent males nearly one in ten is infected with chlamydia. In a report made by Family News in Focus (a Web site of Focus on the Family), Cindy Bailey of the Minnesota Family Institute says, "We continue to tell young people ... that condoms will protect them from sexually transmitted diseases or infections." Then she goes on to say, "That's really not true."[5]
- The average age of a new recruit into teen prostitution is thirteen; some kids are as young as nine. According to the FBI, more and more of these kids are coming from middle-class homes.
- The average teen working within the sex-for-sale industry can easily make $400 for "an evening of fun." What concerns child advocates is that teen prostitutes don't engage in illicit sex for the money but for the thrill of it.
- According to the teens and preteens surveyed, one of the most significant influences in early sexual activity is the media.
- American children spend more than thirty-eight hours a week being entertained by the media, which include music, television, movies, periodicals, and computers.

Think about it: thirty-eight hours a week. That's nearly what the average working American puts in "on the clock." In that amount of time, multiplied by fifty-two weeks, the average

American adolescent will see approximately 14,000 sexual images. Out of that number, roughly 165 will reference birth control, self-control, abstinence, pregnancy, or STDs.[6]

Only 165 out of 14,000.

The statistic that turned my stomach more than all the others combined (and you will be reading quite a few of them within these pages) is this: in the last five years, the rate of porn increased 1800 percent.[7]

I quoted this statistic during a recent radio interview. The interviewer was silent for a full five seconds before continuing. "Eva Marie," he said, "that's a gigantic number." I agreed that it was. "How are we supposed to fight a giant like that?" he asked. I could hear the absolutely flabbergasted tone in his voice.

I immediately pictured young David—the boy who would one day be the king of Israel—standing in the middle of an open field, facing down the giant Goliath.

CONSIDER THIS

You may think you know the story of David and Goliath well, but take a few moments to read the following excerpts from 1 Samuel 17:

> David said to Saul, "Let no one lose heart on account of this Philistine; your servant will go and fight him."
>
> Saul replied, "You are not able to go out against this Philistine and fight him; you are only a boy, and he has been a fighting man from his youth."
>
> But David said to Saul, "Your servant has been keeping his father's sheep. When a lion or a bear came and carried off a sheep from the flock, I went after it, struck it and rescued the sheep from its mouth. When it turned on me, I seized it by its hair, struck it and killed it.... The LORD who delivered me from the paw of the lion and the paw of the bear will deliver me from the hand of this Philistine."
>
> Saul said to David, "Go, and the LORD be with you."

Then Saul dressed David in his own tunic. He put a coat of armor on him and a bronze helmet on his head. David fastened on his sword over the tunic and tried walking around, because he was not used to them.

"I cannot go in these," he said to Saul, "because I am not used to them." So he took them off. Then he took his staff in his hand, chose five smooth stones from the stream, put them in the pouch of his shepherd's bag and, with his sling in his hand, approached the Philistine....

David said to the Philistine, "You come against me with sword and spear and javelin, but I come against you in the name of the LORD Almighty, the God of the armies of Israel, whom you have defied.... All those gathered here will know that it is not by sword or spear that the LORD saves; for the battle is the LORD's, and he will give all of you into our hands."

As the Philistine moved closer to attack him, David ran quickly toward the battle line to meet him. Reaching into his bag and taking out a stone, he slung it and struck the Philistine on the forehead. The stone sank into his forehead, and he fell facedown on the ground.

So David triumphed over the Philistine with a sling and a stone; without a sword in his hand he struck down the Philistine and killed him. (1 Sam. 17:32–35, 37–40, 45, 47–50)

Within the story of David and Goliath, there are lessons of strength to be used in the war against Satan's desire to steal your children.

1. For the sake of your children, do not lose hope!

2. Saul's declaration that the giant was too great for little David to fight may ring true in your own ears. Porn is up 1800 percent in the past five years. How can we fight it? Like David, without fear and with faith!

3. David's declaration that he had been tending his father's sheep is a reminder to us, as mothers and fathers, that we have been tending the "little lambs" that God, our heavenly Father,

gave to us. They are ours. They do not belong to the lion or the bear. We have protected them from the little evils in the world since the day they were born. We fed them when they were hungry, changed them when they were wet or dirty, watched them closely while they played at the park, kissed boo-boos from their falling down, taught them about "proper touching," steered them away from the neighborhood bully, took great care in choosing their schools and childcare, and above all made certain that they were exposed to the Word of God from the moment of their birth. We have already fought a number of battles concerning them, whether we realize it or not.

4. Just as David could not fight Goliath with worldly armor, so we will be most unsuccessful if we try to fight this battle "the world's way." According to advocacy groups, if we don't want our teen and preteen daughters pregnant, we should pass out birth control. If we don't want our teen and preteen sons to contract an STD, we should pass out condoms. No! What we should do is put the armor of the living God around them. Tell them the truth! Tell them the truth about pregnancy, STDs, and—above all—how sex robs them of future intimacy with their wife or husband and currently robs them of intimacy with God.

5. Don't just talk to your children. Talk to God! Pray every single day over the lives of your children. Don't begin praying when the trouble starts. Pray from the moment you are certain of their being. Pray against the work of the Enemy. Pray a hedge of protection around them. Pray specifically about their walk with the love of a lifetime—Jesus.

6. Run to the battle line! Meet the "giant" head-on with the weapon you have "in your hand," which is the truth. You are literally armed with the power of the Holy Spirit of God. Jesus said, "You will know the truth, and the truth will set you free" (John 8:32). The truth is twofold as it pertains to this book. First, tell them the truth about Jesus, about his will for their lives,

Society expects far too much from our educators without even knowing what actually happens each day in our schools.

—G. W. (Bill) Reynolds III, *Sin City*[8]

about his desire for relationship with them. Tell them daily how important they are to him. Show them the Scriptures that deal with their minds, their lives, and God's will for their sexuality. Remind them of James 4:7, which reads, "Submit yourselves, then, to God. Resist the devil, and he will flee from you." Second, tell them the truth about what the media are saying to them. This will require your knowing what the media are saying to them. Don't expect that your son's or daughter's school will "educate" them in these areas. That's not their job. It's your job. You are the shepherd who guards the sheep. You are the warrior facing down the giant. You are the parent, and these are your children.

7. Remember, Satan has already lost the ultimate war. When it comes to the lives of your children, don't allow him to win any battles without putting up one hellacious fight.

CHAPTER 2

Do You Hear What I Hear?

Music, Sex, and Your Children

They had as king over them the angel of the Abyss, whose name in Hebrew is Abaddon, and in Greek, Apollyon.

—REVELATION 9:11

It is the last Sunday in January. As always, my husband and I are in the company of our friends, their children and grandchildren, at the home of Bob and Liz, whom we affectionately call "Moose and Squirrel," all gathered together to watch the Super Bowl on television. Squirrel is a fabulous cook, so as my husband and I drive the few miles between our home and theirs, we anticipate all the goodies we will be munching on soon. When we arrive, true to form, Squirrel is stirring a large pot of homemade soup while Moose is out on the terrace in the backyard, grilling sausages and ribs on the built-in barbecue.

The night is perfect. The weather is cool but not cold. Moose has lit a fire in the outdoor fireplace, and several of us gather around to sip our drinks and nibble on ribs. Someone announces the beginning of the ball game, and the men move to an outside TV. A few women gather as well, though most of us retreat to the kitchen, where we'll sit around the table, drink coffee, and slice "Super Bowl" cake. Most of the children—some as old as eighteen, others as young as six—camp out on the floor of the living room, right in front of the big screen. We comment on the singer chosen to sing the National Anthem. We hear the roar of the crowd. Every so often, laughter emits from outside: another commercial has been enjoyed.

After a while—a nice, long while—someone calls out, "Halftime!"

This is the moment we'd all been waiting for—the halftime show with Janet Jackson as the "star." Earlier that week a news release had promised "shocking moments."

Most of us assume that Michael* will be showing up. "This ought to be a phenomenal show of talent," I think, so I push myself away from the coffee and cake and mosey on into the living room, where I stand behind the centrally located sofa.

Directly in front of me sit a boy and girl, both about ten years of age.

I can't believe what I'm seeing. I'm trying to be cool—after all, I'm in a room full of teens and kids and a splattering of adults. I don't necessarily recognize the singers and dancers—they aren't of my generation—but I know enough to furrow my brow. "What are they doing?" I wonder.

And then the big moment comes. Janet, backed by nearly thirty dancers, sings and dances in a costume reflective of a dominatrix. Her surprise guest is not her brother, but Justin Timberlake, who was at one time with boy band *NSYNC.

A "suggestive duet" it's been called. As Justin sings the line "I'm gonna have you naked by the end of this song" (from his song "Rock Your Body"), he turns slightly to the right, reaches across himself and Janet with his left hand, and pulls away the portion of her costume covering her right breast.

My eyes widen.

"Whoa!" the young boy below me calls out, laughing.

"Was that real?" I think, turning and walking out of the room. I honestly can't think of anything to say.

By the next day, the rest of the world was abuzz. More than 143 million viewers were either aghast or a-giggling. The

*The authors are expressing their opinion of the Jacksons' talent and not of their personal lives.

Federal Communications Commission (FCC) launched an immediate investigation. Both CBS and MTV (Music Television) were scrambling for the right words of apology. Justin issued two statements, one contrary to the other. Janet, a few days later, gave her apologetic explanation. Ironically, in her first interview after the Super Bowl incident (on the *CBS Late Show* with David Letterman), Janet was bleeped for using the J-word.

In this case, J was not for Janet or Jackson or "Just-Doing-My-Own-Thang." J was for "Jesus," used as a swear word, rather than the Name above all names.

And parents—both Christian and non-Christian—struggled to explain to their children the point of the whole display.

Ironically, that one shocking moment did more for the cause of decency than all the soapbox speeches from all the conservatives combined. Even those parents who claim no deep spiritual convictions are now cautious about what their children see and hear in the media.

Or are they? And are those of us who call ourselves "Christian," for that matter? Just how much do we really know about today's music and its influence on our children?

Consider This

The top songs of 1960 included "I'm Sorry" (sung by Brenda Lee), "Are You Lonesome Tonight" (sung by Elvis Presley), and "Teen Angel" (sung by Mark Dinning).

Among the top songs of 1970 were "Bridge Over Troubled Water" (sung

You knew what kind of entertainment you were selling, and you wanted us all to be abuzz here in this room and on the playground of my kid's school because it improves your ratings, it improves your market share, and it lines your pockets.

—Rep. Heather Wilson, R-NM, after the 2004 Super Bowl halftime show[1]

Elvis might have shook his pelvis, but he never showed it to anybody.

—Lewis Grizzard, Southern humorist[2]

by Simon and Garfunkel), "Ain't No Mountain High Enough" (sung by Diana Ross), and "I'll Be There" (sung by the Jackson Five).

A decade later, new trends were emerging. Still, songs like "Call Me" (sung by Blondie), "Another One Bites the Dust" (sung by Queen, one of the first bands to openly declare their alternative lifestyle), and "Rock with You" (sung by Michael Jackson) raised few eyebrows.

Then, in 1984, an album was released that would soon change it all. Madonna's "Like a Virgin" single and video influenced fashion and even the way little girls viewed themselves. It wasn't so much older teen girls who were emulating her, but rather preteen girls. Everywhere one looked, ten- and eleven-year-old girls had taken on the icon's style and image.

In all honesty, Madonna's wasn't the first hint of sex in music. Songs like "Lay, Lady, Lay" (Bob Dylan) and "Lola" (The Kinks) rocked the sixties. The seventies introduced disco and songs like "Love to Love You, Baby" (Donna Summer). Disco parties coupled with drugs and multiple sex partners were the rage—and outbreaks of genital herpes increased as never before.

There is nothing new under the sun.

As a parent, you may have been a part of that lifestyle. Or you may have been too young to remember it. But you probably remember the eighties and the changes that came about within and from the music industry. If

We all think about sex and love, and I've got songs about both on my record. People gravitate to the sex songs more. Surprise, surprise.

—*NSYNC band member JC Chasez, whose solo album, *Schizophrenic*, contains tunes such as "All Day Long I Dream about Sex" and "One Night Stand"[3]

so, you may be thinking, "Yes, we were pretty radical back then, so I'm sure I can talk to my kids openly and honestly about the way things were."

Attention, parent! Your kids listen to music four to six hours per day on average and are in musical "muck and mire" unlike anything history has ever seen. What you experienced or even what I experienced in the sixties and seventies was but the tip of the sexual revolution iceberg. Children of younger and younger ages are responding to sexuality, thanks, in part, to the music industry.

Recently, while at a birthday party for a friend's seven-year-old daughter, I noted one of the young guests as she responded to a Mary-Kate and Ashley doll. "Oh, cool!" she exclaimed. "Britney Spears!"

"The problem with Britney," my daughter said to me as we researched this section of the book, "is that she sings and performs for adults ... but her audience is children."

True. Britney Spears is considered a "pop icon."

What's a parent to do?

Read on.

PARENTAL WARNINGS

In May 1985, Tipper Gore, wife of then-Senator Al Gore, overheard the lyrics of a song her daughter was listening to.

For her part, Spears has responded to their concerns by stating that she is "not their babysitter. It's the parents' responsibility. If you don't like it, turn the TV off. The only person I want to be a role model is to my sister, Jamie Lynn."[4]

Horrified, she encouraged other wives from Washington's political front to join her in forming the Parents Music Resource Center. The primary goal of PMRC is to advise parents of the new and harmful trends in some of today's music.

In September of that same year, the United States Senate

Commerce, Technology, and Transportation Committee began an investigation into the allegations made by PMRC. Musical artists came to defend their craft, spouting their First Amendment rights.

According to *In Touch* magazine, musical artist Pink has viewed Madonna as a "god" since the age of eight. "If Madonna came to me with her mouth open, I wouldn't know what to do!" Pink adds with a laugh. "Women are very sexy!"[5]

A label known as the "Tipper Sticker" soon found itself on the covers of records that contained offensive content, according to PMRC. Some stores across the country determined that if an album displayed the sticker, they would refuse to sell it at all.

THE HOT 100

The top performers in varying genres of music will change as quickly as *Billboard's* Hot 100. However, a few of the artists have "staying power." The important factor is knowing what the artists stand for, what their music sounds like, how the lyrics read, and so forth. By merely asking your children, you'll probably not get a clear-cut answer. Spend time checking out the music your children listen to.

Here's a suggestion: when taking trips—to school, the market, sporting activities—make a deal. "We'll listen to my favorite music going, and yours on the way home." (Or vice versa.) This will give you an opportunity to hear what your children find entertaining and enjoyable.

Another idea. Simply look at the CDs on your children's shelf, lying on the floor, scattered in the closet, and so forth. Take the time to read the lyrics of the songs on them. Certainly do not try to read something into them that's not there, but do look for underlying messages, especially as they pertain to sex, violence, drug usage, and so forth.

THE RIPPLE AND THE WAVE OF HIP-HOP

Let me give you three *h*'s to think about: hip, hop, and hot.

Hip-hop is hot. Sizzling hot—and it doesn't really matter whether your children are African American or not; they are listening to it.

Now, you may say, "Hold on a minute. I've checked all the CDs in my children's collection, and not one hip-hop disc can be found." That may be true, but let me ask you this: Are your children watching television? Have you noticed lately the number of commercial ads that use hip-hop music as a background for the selling of their goods? If a child is enticed by the beat to buy the next coolest pair of sneakers, the result is a new fan of hip-hop.

If you want to know something about their [children's] world, get to know their music.

—Jessica Everson

As a parent you should be aware that if your children are drawn to the music, they will ultimately become interested in the videos, many of which feature porn stars, excessive violence, blatant sexuality, and—for me, the most disturbing—an image of women as primarily playthings for men.

Through her music, her God and her God-fearing man whom she plans to marry in the coming months, [Mary J.] Blige has been able to take control of her drama-filled existence ... she has sobered up, found religion and a love of self.

—Kevin Chappell in *Ebony* magazine[6]

TALKING TO YOUR KIDS ABOUT SEX AND THE MUSIC INDUSTRY: EVA MARIE

Remember when life with your children was simple? Remember listening to tunes from Disney movies while traveling in the car, or singing "I'm a Little Teapot" or "Father Abraham"?

When Jessica was moving from her "little girl" years and into her "preteen" years, I wrote a poem about her. In it were the following lines:

> I have heard the sounds
> of lullabies repeated
> of boats rowing gently
> down a stream.
> Itsy Bitsy Spiders
> and Little Teapots short and stout.
> Melodies of children's hymnals
> And nursery rhymes ...
> ... or class slogans ...
> Voices mingling as we sing with the car's radio.
> Fading into songs I don't know ...
> ... I won't know ...
> It's her generation.

I made a serious mistake when my daughter stopped listening exclusively to "my radio station" and "my music." Sure, I allowed her to listen to her music on trips, but I often turned a deaf ear to what I heard, focusing rather on the positive attributes. Nice beat. Easy to dance to.

But this wasn't *American Bandstand*, and my daughter wasn't just anybody's child. She was mine, and I wanted the best for her. (Jessica may have a different viewpoint on this subject, which you will read shortly.) For a while, I was deeply concerned about the effects of the music I was hearing, but I wasn't sure I knew enough to approach the subject. After all, if I were to talk about Eminem's music and style (for example), she could easily come back with, "But, Mother, he's the parent of a little girl too."

After a little research I soon discovered it was true. But I also read these words from his song "My Dad's Gone Crazy": "I don't blame you, I wouldn't let Hailie [his daughter, Hailie Jade Mathers] listen to me neither."[7]

I hope this book will keep you from feeling the same way. So let's look at a few things I've learned by trial and error. First and foremost, remember that music is often reflective of what your children are feeling inside. If the music tends to be upbeat, they most likely are too. If the music is dark and depressive, they probably are too. If your children are listening to music about peer pressure, rejection, and abuse, there's a good chance they are having problems at school. Teens will gravitate toward the music that speaks the loudest to their souls.

Here are some tips on how to deal with this kind of situation.

1. Listen to the music; listen to the lyrics. Then talk to your children about your concerns. Have all your facts (including the scriptural ones) before having a "meeting of the minds" with them.

2. When talking to your children, don't forget the music of your own youth. It may be easy to become self-righteous until you go back and study some of the lyrics on your dusty albums, dilapidated eight-tracks, and warped cassette tapes.

3. Don't lecture your children. Listen to what they have to say. When they know they can trust you not to "blow your top," they will feel freer to open up.

4. If you find lyrics that are disturbing, express your feelings without the quintessential "because I said so." Show them not only the biblical implications, but also the social and moral implications.

5. Help your children find options. They probably won't be happy about your "dictating what they can and cannot listen to," and that's okay. As a concerned parent, in this situation your purpose is not to make friends; your purpose is to raise children. Remind them that there is a difference between censorship and freedom of expression.

6. Remind your children that music's interpretation of sex and reality is often distorted and/or unrealistic. If lyrics suggest vile and violent actions toward women and you are talking to your son, ask him, "Is this the way you'd want someone to talk about your sister? Your mother? Your future wife?" If you are talking to your daughter, ask her, "Is this the way you want a man—any man—to treat you?"

7. Give your children biblical truths concerning the absolute beauty of intimacy between a husband and wife. Tell them, "This is God's gift to the bride and groom, and it is not to be opened before the wedding night." Don't be afraid to get real with your children about all aspects of this truth. Music makers and singers aren't. You shouldn't be either.

8. Remember that your children are bombarded by sexual images and messages from music every day. What you do to combat that situation (in other words, your example) is critical. Children report across the board that their parents are their number one influence. Keep that fact in mind as you are listening to your own tunes. If you hear something that goes against what you believe, turn to your children and say, "You know, I have to admit that those words go against what I believe." Then talk about it, and be willing to change the channel or track.

9. If you or your children have purchased music you find distasteful, take it back to the store. Talk to the manager about why you are doing so. Don't be shy. These are your children.

10. Remember to supervise more than just the music your children purchase from the store. Monitor the music they download from the Internet as well.

11. Consider forming a parents' group. Meet monthly. Discuss the latest in trends, the top 100, and so forth. Get informed! Stay informed. Purchase magazines like *Rolling Stone,* and read what's going on. Go to Web sites like True Lies (www.truelies.org), Center for Parent/Youth Understanding

(www.cpyu.org), and Morality in
Media, Inc. (obscenitycrimes.org) for
further information.

TALKING TO YOUR KIDS ABOUT SEX AND THE MUSIC INDUSTRY: JESSICA

Music is an absolutely beautiful gift of
God that, not unlike any other gift
from God, has been perverted by the
devil. Its beauty and perfection are still
quite evident though, and, as one of
the greatest loves of my heart, I thank
God daily for sharing it with me. He

When asked by Regis
Philbin on his show
*Live! with Regis and
Kelly* what her father
(who is a Baptist
pastor) thought of the
language used on her
show, newlywed
Jessica Simpson
replied with a smile,
"He's loosening up."[9]

has blessed us all with its power. Because of it I have been moved
beyond the capacity of words by a multitude of great artists and
musical pieces. Each one has left me filled with a happiness and
an abundance of other emotions with which most earthly things
cannot begin to compare.

On the flip side, I have also found that more and more music
is being used by the devil to be the carrier of his themes and projects of immorality. With the power of music on his side, he is
reaching souls and minds by the billions.

Possibly one of the biggest mistakes you can make concerning your children's music is closing your ears to any artist
or song or type of music (or opinion for that matter) that your
children respect or love simply because of the negative aspect,
characteristic, quality, or attribute that you find in it. Of course
you can do so if you want to. You can call it filth, close your
mind completely, refuse to listen, and spout off doctrine till
you are blue in the face—and you may feel totally justified in
doing so. But you must understand that what's important now
is not what's morally right or wrong, or even your opinion. It's
your children's opinions, and what they decide is okay for

them, that is of primary concern. All you should expect to gain from your closed mind is the same from your children toward you and the values and beliefs you hold dear. And all you will then be able to monitor is the time when they are under your complete supervision. Mind you, the rules do vary depending on the age and situation of your children; but when they reach the point where you can no longer control what they listen to every second of the day, and they've begun to develop their own taste in music, what I am suggesting here should remain relevant.

What you must understand is that your children need you now more than ever. They need you to teach them how to be grown-ups. They need you to guide them through the messed-up reality they've been given by the same ones who hold the responsibility to ensure their well-being. And let me assure you that your example helps them to be salmon swimming against a current so fierce that it threatens to pull them under at any given moment. Though we all fall short often, every single one of us who is no longer a child has been given the responsibility to teach our youth by example "the way they should go." (See Prov. 22:6.)

This is true not just for your children, but for all children. (Remember the days when the whole neighborhood and community participated in the rearing of a child?) Don't take me wrong; I am definitely not laying the weight of the entire state of the world on your shoulders. I am just pointing out the often forgotten fact that if you're a woman and your children are girls, or if you're a man and your children are boys, no matter what your relationship, automatically they become your students. But what happens when you're not your children's only teacher?

First, do not be discouraged and feel that your lessons will be lost among all the other information they will receive. Let me assure you that your children will look to you first and foremost throughout their lives for their examples of how young ladies and young gentlemen should live, even when it seems that they couldn't care less about your opinion. This means that the basis of their faith and acceptance in what you teach them is your ability to lead by example on a daily basis. And the smallest things will count. I recall the days when I was growing up; when I would try to avoid certain phone calls, my parents would never lie for me and say that I wasn't home. Whether or not I agreed with their decision, that is something I often refer to. I know it is things like that that helped to mold my character.

The other factor that will affect your level of influence is your willingness to be open and honest with your children about the things they see going on around them, and sometimes about your own experiences. The sad truth of it is, our youth have been losing their faith in the very institutions we were taught to rely on. The government, the school system, the police, even the church are filled with stories of greed, hypocrisy, deceit, selfishness, political corruption, oppression, and immorality. I mean no disrespect, but we are witnesses to all these things. This is why our youth—now more than ever— find it difficult to connect faith to any religion or specific doctrine, while completely connecting to music and the messages it brings. I think it is important that you understand and respect this situation for your children's sake, because they need you to meet them where they are, not where you are, in order to explain their view of the world, not your own.

I promise that you cannot seclude them from what you don't like for them if they can't understand for themselves why your action is best for them. First of all, it's impossible, unless they never leave their closet; and second, you will wind up pushing them right toward the things you are trying to protect them from. Take for example Scott Stapp, the lead singer of the band Creed, whose "secular" lyrics are often filled with lines of redemption, salvation, and theology. His Christian mother actually forbade him to listen to any kind of rock music, even Christian rock.

So how can you reach your children and open up the lines of communication so that you can help influence the decisions they make for themselves when you are not around? Let's first talk about why music speaks so strongly to young people. I made a list of some of the main reasons I believe today's youth are so connected with their music.

1. It meets them where they are.
2. It accepts them as they are.
3. It expresses the things they can't, don't, or won't express for themselves.
4. It answers their questions without their having to ask.
5. It finds commonality with them through situations and emotions.
6. It tells their story.
7. It makes them feel good about their world.
8. It makes them proud of their world.
9. It makes them feel good about themselves.
10. It can be a temporary escape.

I think you would do well to try to imitate some of these characteristics. I believe this is possible to do without giving up your own beliefs or accepting the choices you don't agree with. Being empathetic and informed about your children's tastes in music does not mean that you have to allow them to listen to the music you don't approve of; but honestly, with technology as it is, unless they make the decision for themselves, your efforts are in vain. That's why I stress that you should focus more on what they want to listen to than what they are allowed to listen to.

Still, it is important that you let your choices for them be known (nonjudgmentally) so that your positive example remains consistent and intact. But be prepared to face the fact that, coming from different experiences, they may view a lot of lyrical content differently from you. They may insist on the positive aspect of music you find appalling, or, at the least, they may try to justify it. But it is very important that you really try to understand "where they are coming from." This understanding begins with listening with them to their favorite music. Don't be afraid to ask about the lyrics or their meaning if you don't understand them. A lot of today's music is filled with slang that could be missed or misunderstood by a parent. You'll most likely find that your children are very willing to discuss the lyrics with you. Otherwise, their silence is probably an indication that there is most definitely a problem with the music in question. Just realize that if they feel okay with the content of a song, it is obviously for a reason, so how can you expect to influence them with your beliefs if you don't even know why it appeals to them so much?

You may be surprised at times to find that they have a valid point. Don't forget that God speaks to and through many different people, not just those who daily walk "the straight and narrow," and that even in the Christian market there sometimes exists scandal. Regardless, if you don't understand what your children believe and why they believe it, how can you expect them to understand when you stress your beliefs to them?

Let me explain another condition that often exists. Suppose children are brought up in a Christian home and taught always about wrong and right, black and white. Then one day when those children have grown a little older, they start to have feelings, thoughts, and desires that don't line up with the rules by which they were raised. All the while within the church they see hypocrisy from the very ones who do not accept their ideas. Soon they will begin to search for a place where they are accepted and loved for who they are even in their imperfection, somewhere they won't feel deceived and confused by what goes on around them.

The youth of today are searching for something real. And a lot of us are beginning to find that realness in God himself as our Father rather than in religion. (This situation, however, leaves room for some young people to "put their own spin on things" and make God a matter of convenience.) Often we find the fruit of the Spirit to be more prevalent in the streets than in the church. (It kind of reminds me of Jesus in the marketplace.) This situation can be very confusing. What your kids need is someone to turn to when the going gets tough—someone who knows what they're going through and who supports them 100 percent. Then they can be part of the few who have a positive adult role model, so they won't have to turn elsewhere when they are in need. If you just tell them what to do and what not to do, when they see that they can't control their environment they may become curious, then intrigued, and soon lose respect for your opinion because you "obviously don't know what you're talking about." And if you don't understand their favorite music artists and their fans, your opinion will lose its potency.

Let me give you an example of the danger of losing your influence in the way your children translate the music they listen to. This example also reinforces why your kids need to find for themselves the motivation behind every message they receive in life. Tupac Shakur was a revolutionist and music artist whose lyrics have been both censored and revered for their often violent or sexual nature. He, however, held that they served a necessity in his purpose, because they were a reflection of the things he witnessed, the same things he was trying to combat. Regardless, he still admitted being aware of the potential effect on children and others who did not understand their purpose and meaning as they attempted to mimic the same behaviors he was working to eliminate. Now ten years after his murder, the pace of this trend has only increased as things continue to spin out of control.

You cannot argue or force the truth; the truth must be discovered, and I believe that only God can put it in our hearts. Your job is to raise your children according to the teachings of Jesus and continuously lead by example. Let the light of Jesus in you bring them and hold them to the Lord. On a practical level, you should be involved in their day-to-day lives enough to know as soon as a problem arises. Kids want their parents to hear all the things that are important to them as long as they feel comfortable sharing them. You just need to make yourself available and listen. Once the lines of communication are open and you have the opportunity to really talk, explain to them as best you can that God's words are not arbitrary. Because none of us can see our future the way he does, heeding his commandments will protect us from otherwise inevitable pain. (Most kids think they have the game of life figured out already and don't even realize that they haven't even been dealt all the cards yet. This may be a hurdle for you. Be creative.)

Assure them that this pain will be real. They may already be able to attest to some examples of it, and, if so, it will help support your convictions. If not, share some experiences of your own.

Remind them of their purpose on earth as children of God, and help them and support them as they search for their individual purpose (as almost all teens are doing). This, in itself, will help clear up a lot of the confusion they may have. Teach them that, no matter where life takes them and what mistakes they make, they must never stop praying and trusting in the Lord, because in him is where their hope lies. Above all else, be their ambassador of faith.

TRUE LIES AND THE CENTER FOR PARENT/YOUTH UNDERSTANDING

As we've already established, there is nothing new under the sun, but what's hot continuously changes. In fact, by the time you read this book, the information in it will be dated. However, all is not lost. For those of us who want to stay current, there are organizations that stay on top of the influence of media on today's youth.

One such organization is True Lies, whose president is Phil Chalmers. Phil had always been a big fan of music, mostly negative music, as well as violent and horror movies. As Phil puts it, "I was also into porn like most kids [at that] age. When I became a Christian, I noticed that the media was really impacting the culture, and I could use the topic of media to get kids' attention, and speak to them about God, sex, drugs, violence, and suicide. And so I did."[10]

In 1984 Phil launched True Lies, and it has been going strong for more than twenty years. The organization has more than thirty speakers (with a goal of fifty to a hundred within the next few years) who give presentations at schools and ministries across the country. The presentations take a look at "four main areas of attack on this generation of young people." Also called the "Four Lies," they are

1. Premarital sex is safe, and everyone's doing it.
2. Drugs and alcohol are harmless.
3. Using violence can solve your problems.
4. Suicide is a way to solve your problems.

Each "lie" is countered with "truth," and the presentations are "packed with high-impact graphics and video, and powerful scriptures." The True Lies presentations are complete with follow-up discussion guides.[11]

In addition to a plethora of disturbing facts, figures, updates, and speaker information, the True Lies Web site offers merchandise and music alternatives. (If you like it, then try it.) In addition to books and videos, what I consider to be among the most beneficial tools as both a parent and an adult is the True Lies newsletter, which is sent out every month via email and can be subscribed to simply by going to the Web site www.truelies.org.

In the movie *High Fidelity*, actor John Cusack looks poignantly at the camera and says, "What came first, the music or the misery? People worry about kids playing with guns, or watching violent videos, that some sort of culture of violence will take them over. Nobody worries about kids listening to thousands, literally thousands, of songs about heartbreak, rejection, pain, misery, and loss. Did I listen to pop music because I was miserable? Or was I miserable because I listened to pop music?"[13]

These lines now find themselves at scads of Web sites and set the tone for the beginning of the Center for Parent/Youth Understanding (CPYU) video *More Than Noise*.[14] Walt Mueller, president and founder of the Center for Parent/Youth Understanding (www.cpyu.org), has worked nearly twenty-five years within youth ministry. In addition to the Web site, Walt's organization has produced merchandise designed to help parents and educate youth with the truth, including the award-winning book *Understanding Today's Youth Culture*[15] and *how to use your HEAD to*

In the February 2004 edition of the magazine *YS* (a magazine for young salvationists), reporter Cynthia Davis wrote an article about top-selling Christian rock band Relient K. In it, band member Matt Hoopes says, "In the Bible it says to honor your mother and father. Also as a Christian you are called to treat people with respect and dignity and love. I think that with your parents it is even more so, because it's someone that you're … stuck with."[12]

*guard your **heart**,*[16] an easy 3-D guide to making responsible music choices. Within the pages are questions to help your children make such choices, including "What's the song's main topic and theme?" and "How are human beings portrayed?"

Also in the stock of their parental help resource center is the afore-mentioned video, *More Than Noise,* a six-segment teaching video for parents and youth workers that states

- ■ Music is directive
- ■ Music shapes a teen's world and life view when it comes to
  - Lessons about right and wrong
  - Conflict resolution
  - Materialism
  - Self-value
  - Response to authority
  - Sexuality
  - Love (redefinition)
  - Relational pain and brokenness
  - The source of redemption (whether in sex, money, or power)
  - Spirituality
  - Christianity confusion
- ■ Music is reflective

The video features Mueller sharing the fascinating story of a mother who came to him and, with excitement in her voice, told him that her daughter was now listening to the music artist who "wears the cross and sings about faith." As it turned out, the artist was George Michael (who went public with his homosexuality in 1998 after being arrested for lewd conduct in a men's

The music today controls [the teens] rather than them controlling the music. [Its] greatest power lies in its ability to shape their values, attitudes, and behaviors. It defines truth and reality for kids.

—Walt Mueller in the video *More Than Noise*[17]

public rest room), the album was titled *Faith*, and among its top hits was the song "I Want Your Sex."

This isn't nearly as surprising when you note that only one out of fourteen "born-again" teens lists "Contemporary Christian" as their favorite style of music.[18]

CHAPTER 3

Who's Minding the Children?

TV, Sex, and Your Children

"See that you do not look down on one of these little ones. For I tell you that their angels in heaven always see the face of my Father in heaven."

—MATTHEW 18:10

I'm not going to allow you to spend your entire summer sitting in front of that one-eyed monster!"

These were the words I heard at the end of every school year when I was growing up, dictated by my sweet mother. "We didn't have TV when I was growing up, and we were better for it," she would add. It was only later that I learned her family was the first in their neighborhood to own a television.

But Mother should have saved her fretting for my daughter, her granddaughter. Television in the sixties was a far cry from television today. I tuned in to shows like *Hazel* and *The Donna Reed Show*. Mornings were for watching *Concentration* and *The Dating Game*, TV's predecessor to shows like *The Bachelor, Extreme Dating, Fifth Wheel,* and *Boy Meets Boy*.

Today's parents—to a great degree—are doing something no other generation of parents has done. With a high percentage of mothers working outside the home[1] and enough time constraints to choke a horse, parents are allowing, through television, sexually active teens (both gay and straight and some with a penchant for violence and bribery) into their homes for the purpose of childcare.[2] Today's children have precious little hope of ever considering sex outside of marriage as anything but normal.

THE HISTORY OF SEX AND TV

In 1934, the Hays Office—headed by Will Hays, then president of the Motion Picture Producers and Distributors of America—implemented a new code of standards by which moviemakers would abide. Film content, it declared, would be limited to "wholesome entertainment." It is hard to believe that Americans in those days were worried about the media's influence, but they were. (For a more detailed understanding of the code and the history behind it, see the next chapter of this book: That's Entertainment? Movies, Sex, and Your Children.) As I mentioned in a previous chapter, nudity in film did occur. And who, in those days or even today, could hold a candle to the passion and sensuality of actors such as Rudolph Valentino and Errol Flynn? These men were so "hot," their escapades went beyond the silver screen, spilling over into real life.

The Federal Communications Act of 1934 gave broadcasters the use of broadcast channels as long as they served the "public interest." However, no one defined exactly what that meant. Today, the Communications Act stands as a monument to the mistake of writing into law vaguely worded quid pro quos. Because the act did not define what "public interest" meant, Congress, the courts, and the FCC have spent sixty frustrating years struggling to figure it out.[3]

In 1947 RCA sold 170,000 seven-inch television sets. Two short years later, more than a million sets were purchased. The following year, television proved it would not be a temporary fad; nearly ten million sets were being viewed and enjoyed in the United States alone. If yours was not one of the households with a set, you only had to go down to the local appliance store to watch or take a stroll to the home of the nearest neighbor who owned one. Owning a television guaranteed friends.

But how did one know who had a set? Simple: a large antenna graced the rooftop of the owner's house. Unlike that which today's youth is accustomed to—remotes and satellites— TV owners in those days changed the channel by getting up, crossing the room, and manually switching channels, followed by adjusting the antenna—if they had an inside antenna remote. (If I sit still long enough, I can still hear the quiet roar as our old antenna remote moved from N to SW.) But let's say a TV owner did not have a remote. In that case, someone in the family had to go outside and literally move the antenna while someone else hollered directions from inside.

In these early years, each week broadcasters aired nearly thirty hours of commercial programs designed for kids. Why? Even then—before TV had made its mark on America—the decision makers knew that to entice parents to buy, they had to entice kids to watch. The more kids watched, the more commercials were necessary. The more commercials, the more products sold. The more products that were sold, the happier the executives. Even when American family values were as wholesome as apple pie, children—those very precious gifts given by God—were considered nothing more than a commodity by television moguls. It is important to understand that one fact before you can truly understand the rest of what I am about to share with you.

To prepare myself for writing this chapter, I read stacks of books. One of the first things I noted as being similar within the words and pages was that money talks; in fact, it does more than just talk—money rules. In his book *The Other Parent*, James P. Steyer, founder and chairman of JPKids (a family and educational media company), states, "While I've met many people in the kids' media industry, both creative types and executives, who do ... care deeply about children, it's at best a minority viewpoint. What I learned the hard way is a very sobering lesson: market forces and the short-term profit goals of a few giant media corporations ... dominate the media world.... Simply put,

If you think TV doesn't have drawing power, think again. On January 19, 1953, 86 percent of all television sets in the United States were tuned in to watch *I Love Lucy*. It was a momentous occasion: Lucy Ricardo was giving birth to "Little Ricky."[5]

money rules all, not the best interest of our kids or our broader society."[4]

The second thing I noted is that sex sells, although this was hardly a shock. What was shocking is that sex sells to kids.

The third thing I noted is that no one seems to care. It's a lot like the weather—everyone talks about it, but no one does anything to change it. Like the weather, we think it's bigger than we are. We don't see "the power of one."

Allow me to share this "power of one" story with you. While watching early morning TV (when children also could be watching while eating their breakfasts before heading off to school), I was a bit unnerved by a herbal weight-loss commercial. Literally nothing was left to the imagination. The actress had "lost weight," looked good, knew she looked good, and if her mirror had been the only witness to it, so be it. But more than her mirror was witness to her new size and shape. I was both witness to it and appalled by it. I went to the company's Web site, found a contact email address, and wrote a letter of complaint. Within two hours I received a reply from the company's representative, who apologized. That commercial was only to be aired late night, during "adult" television. The representative asked for the station I had been watching, vowing to contact it. I answered the email, providing the information requested. Later that day I received another email, assuring me that I would never see that commercial during a time slot when children might be viewing. The message stated, "Exposure of our advertisements to children is a critical concern." At the end of the correspondence, I was thanked profusely for letting the company know.

A similar incident, however, left me black and blue, bruised emotionally. When I called the network, I was in no uncertain terms informed that the advertisers simply didn't care what I thought or had to say. Those I spoke with were downright rude. I suppose that's the risk we take when we exert our "power of one" status, but it is a risk worth taking.

You Say You Want a Revolution

In 1961 Newton Minow, having just been named chairman of the Federal Communications Commission (FCC), shocked America when he told the nation's television broadcasters that, in his opinion, they had turned television into a "vast wasteland." In the opening lines of his book *Abandoned in the Wasteland*, cowritten with Craig L. LaMay, Minow begins by telling how the idea for the book came about. In 1991 he had been invited to analyze what had occurred within the "wasteland" in the thirty years since he had made his original and often-quoted statement. His conclusion was that while TV had more choices than in the sixties, the "wasteland had only grown vaster."[7]

Out of the 14,000 sexual images seen by your child this year, three-fourths will come from television. Find that difficult to believe? Turn on the television for one hour and watch.[6]

Ah, the sixties. In those days nearly everyone had a television—and, as today, the generation itself pretty much derived its identity from what it saw on the more popular shows. Among them were the following:

AMERICAN BANDSTAND

American Bandstand could be called a "reality/variety show" of sorts. It actually began in the 1950s but reigned in the sixties as a weekly, one-hour show starring Dick Clark as the host to a growing-in-popularity group of teens, who danced to the latest tunes and then welcomed currently "hot" guests, who sang their newest releases. It was clean and, above all, fun and entertaining.

THE ANDY GRIFFITH SHOW

Homespun humor and law and order were kept as top priorities in the fictitious town of Mayberry, North Carolina, from 1960 to 1968. Sheriff Andy Taylor, Deputy Barney Fife, Aunt Bea Taylor, and Andy's son, Opie Taylor, were among the beloved townspeople who gave the airwaves lessons for living. The strongest language ever heard on the show was "fiddle-faddle!"

THE LUCY SHOW

Everyone loved Lucy. Lucille Ball began her TV career as one of the first leading ladies of the small screen in *I Love Lucy*, which starred then-husband Desi Arnaz as bandleader Ricky Ricardo and featured regulars Vivian Vance and William Frawley as their best friends Fred and Ethel Mertz. In those days husbands and wives (even the ones married in "real life") weren't allowed to share a bed on TV, and women didn't become ... er ... pregnant. However, when Mrs. Arnaz did indeed become pregnant, the obvious solution was to have "Mrs. Ricardo" be "with child" as well. But did you know that a local priest, rabbi, and minister were brought in as consultants to assure producers and others that there was nothing objectionable about the pregnancy installments?[8] When *I Love Lucy* went off the air, *The Lucy Show* took its place, featuring Ms. Ball as a bumbling secretary, but a successful single, who lived in Los Angeles. Though single-in-the-city, she never once had a man stay the night or went out and got smashed. In spite of this situation, her show continues to be enjoyed in reruns to this day.

GUNSMOKE

In the sixties even little girls loved a good Western, and I was no exception. One of my favorites was *Gunsmoke*, which ran for twenty action-packed years (1955–1975) and can easily be called the granddaddy of all Westerns. Set in Dodge City, Kansas, during the late 1800s, the show featured U.S. Marshal Matt Dillon, Deputy Chester Goode (later replaced by Festus Hagin), saloon owner "Miss Kitty" Russell, and "Doc" Adams, the beloved characters who survived the changes endured in the post–Civil War Midwest. While everyone wondered about the relationship between Dillon and Russell, the two never shared even a peck on the lips. Maybe that's what kept us tuning in.

DRAGNET

"Dum de dum dum …" (theme song). "My name's Friday." "Just the facts, ma'am." "It's my job; I'm a cop." *Dragnet* was the half-hour police drama featuring Joe Friday and Bill Gannon, a couple of tight-lipped Los Angeles detectives who solved true crimes. ("The story you have just seen is true. Only the names have been changed to protect the innocent.") Every detective show since owes some form of gratitude to its creator and star, Jack Webb, and his portrayal of a serious, good cop.

Pop sensation Madonna allows her children, Lourdes and Rocco, to watch no TV and only one DVD a week "as a treat."[9]

NEARING THE END OF AN AGE

The Children's Television Act did not become law until 1990. This act marked the first time Congress recognized children as a special audience, and it required commercial broadcasters to provide "educational and informational" programs for children. Until recently, however, broadcasters all but ignored the law.[10]

In the Telecommunications Act of 1996, Congress gave the industry its first opportunity to establish voluntary ratings. The industry established a system, also known as "TV Parental Guidelines," for rating programming that contains sexual, violent, or other material parents may deem inappropriate, and committed to voluntarily broadcast signals containing these ratings, which are displayed on the television screen for the first fifteen seconds of rated programming. The ratings are as follows, all preceded with "TV":

Y—Appropriate for all children.

Y7—Appropriate for children ages seven and above.

G—Appropriate for general audiences.

PG—Parental guidance suggested. May contain "V" (violence), "S" (sexual situations), "L" (coarse language), or "D" (suggestive dialogue).

14—Parents strongly cautioned. May contain material inappropriate for children under the age of fourteen. May also contain V, S, L, or D.

MA—Mature audiences only. Contains V, S, or L.

These guidelines do not pertain to sports and news, and both NBC and BET (Black Entertainment Network) refused to use the system in its entirety, stating that the new system would have a negative effect. Some programmers use voice-overs to state, "The following program may contain material not suitable for young children. Parental discretion is advised." This is good, of course, except that nowadays it is heard so much that many parents have adapted their mind's ears to it and may not do anything about it. Instead they may feel that if anything happens they don't approve of, they will simply ask their children to leave the room, or they will change the channel. The problem with this mentality is that once an image in seared into a child's mind, it remains there.

In carrying out the new act, all sets thirteen inches or larger manufactured after January 1, 2000, were required to have V-chip technology. This computer chip (named V for Violence), built into the television's technology, allows parents to determine what they wish their children to view.

Though 90 percent of parents surveyed support a rating system for television, only 7 percent use the V-chip monitor. Why? When surveyed, they said they don't know how to use it. How can this be? How can a generation of parents who sport cell phones and Palm Pilots, own PCs and laptops, and have every possible form of technology in their homes be intimidated by this tiny form of child protection?

Yet approximately 85 to 90 percent of American parents believe that the media contribute to children becoming too materialistic, use more coarse and vulgar language, engage in sexual activity at younger ages, experience a premature loss of innocence, and behave in violent or antisocial ways.[11]

Parents cite television (37 percent) as having the most negative impact.

The best estimate is that parents watch TV with their younger children (ages two to seven) about 19 percent of the children's total TV time and that they almost never watch with "tweens" (youngsters ages nine through twelve) and teens.[12]

THE NEW AGE OF TELEVISION

Yep, the times they are a-changin', as folk singer Bob Dylan once crooned.

I recently received a phone call from a distraught parent. "Eva Marie," she said, "I want to be honest with you. When I was a kid, I managed to sneak into an X-rated movie ... but I have to tell you; what I saw there was tame compared to what I saw the other night on television." She was speaking specifically about *Nip/Tuck*, a show being highly hailed by critics as the hottest thing on television. *Nip/Tuck* is also a show that leaves nothing to the imagination as it deals with deviant sexual behavior between same-sex couples and both single and married adults.

Three out of four teens say the fact that "TV shows and movies make it seem normal for teenagers to have sex" is one reason teenagers have sex.[13]

So how did we get to this place?

Between 1965 and 2002, the amount of time American kids spent with their parents dropped 40 percent, the difference between thirty hours per week and seventeen. What are they doing instead? Predominately they are engaging themselves in the media.

In February 2001, a report headed by Dr. Dale Kunkel, a leading expert on children's media policy to the Kaiser Family Foundation, was released. In it was published the results of a study done on the distribution of sexual messages on television, 1998 versus 2000. The following was reported:

In 1998, 56 percent of programs had sexual content. By 2000, it had jumped to 68 percent. In 1998, 54 percent of programs "talked about" sex. By 2000, that number had jumped to 65 percent. In 1998, sex scenes involving teens was 3 percent, with the two-year jump being 9 percent. Put another way, only three scenes featured teen intercourse across the entire composite week in 1998, while sixteen such scenes occurred in 2000.[14]

Remember that, since that report and at the time of this writing, another four years have passed.

Welcome to the new millennium. Television just isn't what it used to be, whether you grew up watching in the fifties, sixties, seventies, or eighties. Television programming now looks like this:

REALITY SHOWS

Reality shows and MTV—the two just go hand in hand. MTV gave birth to shows like *Cribs*, *Real World*, and *The Osbournes*, which went on to become the highest-rated series in cable history. Not only was it popular with adults, but it was nearly a staple with teens. So on the off chance that you have been living on another planet, here's the scoop. *The Osbournes*—Ozzy, wife Sharon, and kids Kelly and Jack—allowed MTV cameras to record typical days spent in their Beverly Hills home. Hailed as a normal family, they were like no family I know. Within the first show, the participants' natural words of conversation were "bleeped" out about sixty times. The children did not live the typical teen lifestyle of school and friends, and the parents were hardly Ozzie and Harriett or even Dan and Roseanne.

FAMILY SHOWS

No, *The Osbournes* aren't it. And, we've also seen a move in what viewers think when they hear the word "family." George, Elaine, Kramer, and Jerry (of *Seinfeld*) were a family of sorts. So were Joey, Ross, Chandler, Monica, Phoebe, and Rachel on *Friends*. The good news is that there are still some positive nuclear family shows on television. Examples at the time of this writing are *The George Lopez Show, 7th Heaven*, and *8 Simple Rules for Dating My Teenage Daughter*.

SINGLE IN THE CITY

Undoubtedly no such show has held popularity in the last few years like *Sex and the City*, which features newspaper columnist Carrie Bradshaw and her three friends Samantha, Miranda, and Charlotte. According to the TV Tome Web site, the show "revolves around the lives of four young professional women in search of the perfect relationship ... and orgasm!"[15]

WESTERNS

For a short while, after the demise of *Dr. Quinn, Medicine Woman*, there were no Westerns on television. Recently, HBO released *Deadwood* (tagged "a hell of a place to make your fortune"). *Deadwood* has been touted by the network's Web site as having "unflinching realism, adult themes and wickedly inventive storylines."[16] Warning: This is not a Western for young boys and girls who wear "six-shooters" while viewing.

Two out of every three shows on TV include sexual content. When intercourse is depicted, 10 percent of the couples have just met, and only half are between couples who have established any type of relationship. Ninety percent of sexual content within TV does not mention the risks involved. Eight percent of all shows contain sexual content involving teens, and 20 percent reference waiting or safe sex. Teens having sex on television has tripled in the last two years.

—Teen Health and the Media[17]

BAD BOYS, BAD BOYS

While Westerns dominating the airwaves are a thing of the past (at least for now—and no pun intended), "cop" or "legal" shows are at an all-time high. Unlike the dramas of yesteryear such as *Dragnet, Magnum PI, Cagney and Lacey,* or even *Miami Vice*, these new shows are filled with graphic scenes and adult situations. Today, shows like *Law and Order, Law and Order: SVU* (Special Victims Unit, which typically deals with sexually violent crime), *Law and Order: Criminal Intent, NYPD Blue, Crossing Jordan, Alias, The DA, The Practice, Monk, The District, Jag, Cold Case, CSI: Miami,* and *Hack* are featured on network television.[18] For the most part, and in and of themselves, these are not bad shows ... if you are an adult. As your children mature, you alone should make the decision as to whether or not they are emotionally and spiritually mature enough to handle the content found in many of these shows.

DAYTIME TELEVISION

DISNEY, CARTOON NETWORK, NICK, AND BOOM

Even your youngest viewers may not be safe, but for the most part, they are. Still, as parents (and even grandparents) we should not assume that just because a television show is animated it is safe or that it is totally harmless.

Case in point: *Kim Possible.* I was introduced to KP ("What's the sitch?") by my then five-year-old granddaughter. "Danger or trouble, I'm there on the double," she sang from the backseat of my car.

"What are you singing?" I asked her.

"Kim Possible!" she continued the show's theme song.

"Who or what is a Kim Possible?" I asked.

"She's a girl, see," Jordynn answered. "But she gets the bad guys too."

I decided to watch the show with my little sweetheart. The theme song is good (though I still don't know what a "sitch" is), and the show is about high-tech crime fighting by some animated high school kids. The danger, as far as we parents are concerned, is that Kim dresses sexily and displays a lot of spunk. In fact, while watching together one afternoon, my granddaughter noted that she liked "Kim's style" of clothes.

This remark, of course, prompted a little chitchat between me and my granddaughter. We talked about why she liked the style, what in particular she liked most, and so forth.

Another Disney show you may want to check on is *That's So Raven.* This show is primarily about a young girl named Raven who receives psychic glimpses into the future and then attempts to solve the problems she foresees. And, it should be noted, the actress Raven, who plays Raven Baxter, is twenty years old—not a young teen by any stretch of the word. Therefore, when her videos are played on TDC (The Disney Channel), she most definitely portrays a grown woman with her style (including exposed cleavage) and her moves.

The very popular *Lizzie McGuire*—starring Hilary Duff—is about a middle-school girl who is vivacious and pretty but unable to get the popularity vote from everyone in school. There is an animated Lizzie who periodically comes to the screen to tell viewers what is really going on inside Lizzie's head. *Lizzie* is a favorite show of more than just tweens. Younger children—more often than not, girls—love watching *Lizzie* too.

Boom, short for Boomerang, is a cable network (part of the Cartoon Network) dedicated to old cartoons. If you're a parent or grandparent with a penchant for nostalgia, let me encourage you to check it out (or have your cable company carry it if it doesn't already). There you can introduce your little loved ones to the likes of Quickdraw McGraw, George Jetson, Sylvester and Tweety, Snagglepuss, and—let's never forget—Yogi and BooBoo.

TRASH TALK

When I was a little girl, talk shows were rather tame: *The Mike Douglas Show*, *The Dinah Shore Chevy Show*, and *The Art Linkletter Show*, for example. These were "talk" and "variety" shows combined and the predecessors of today's talk/variety shows. For me, they were and still are entertaining and fun, but today there is another form of "talk" show known as "trash talk," which, in my humble opinion, is neither entertaining nor fun and whose content is an issue mothers and fathers need to be keenly aware of.

The questions at the forefront of my mind as I am writing this chapter are "Why do teens and young adults gravitate toward trash talk shows?" and "How did all this insanity happen?"

In the late sixties, Phil Donahue appeared on the airwaves in *The Phil Donahue Show*, which most folks simply called *Donahue*. *Donahue* was "the precursor to all the daytime talk shows that arose during the 1980s and '90s."[19]

> Phil Donahue established "talk television," an extension of the "hot topic" live radio call-in shows of the 1960s. Donahue himself ran a radio show in Dayton, Ohio before premiering his daytime television talk show. Donahue's Dayton show, later syndicated nationally, featured audience members talking about the social issues that affected their lives.... Talk shows are indeed forums in which society tests out and comes to terms with the topics, issues, and themes that define its basic values, what it means to be a "citizen," a participating member of that society. The "talk television" show of Phil Donahue became a microcosm of society as cutting-edge social and cultural issues were debated and discussed.[20]

The 1980s introduced other talk shows, including *Sally Jessy Raphael*, *Geraldo*, and the talk show of all talk shows, *The Oprah Winfrey Show*.

Meanwhile, there was a growing dance between the push to sex and violence in these shows—packaged as romance and domestic conflict in the shows primarily for women, as lust and aggression in the shows primarily for men—and the opposing forces of morality and decency.[21] As the decade progressed, talk show producers became less interested in the tell-all lives of celebrities and more interested in the tell-all lives of the people next door. They wanted to appeal to a younger audience—including teens. As the eighties moved on toward the nineties, talk show formats were "a mix of celebrities, ordinary people drawn into the headlines of the day, and experts knowledgeable about a topic."[22] By the end of the eighties, talk

TV producers began to look for the most bizarre stories they could find.

And find them, they did.

It can easily be stated that no incident raised more eyebrows as to the dangers involved in these types of shows than the "Jenny Jones incident." On March 6, 1995, the once-popular talk show, *The Jenny Jones Show*, hosted by its namesake, aired an episode titled "Same Sex Secret Crushes." On the show, Jonathan Schmitz listened as Ms. Jones described someone who had a secret crush on him. When the mystery guest was revealed, it turned out to be Schmitz's neighbor, thirty-two-year-old Scott Amadeur. Schmitz's face registered surprise, but everything seemed to be cool when the two left the show, still friends. Three days after the airing of the show, however, Schmitz shot and killed Amadeur with a twelve-gauge shotgun. What followed was a trial in which Schmitz was convicted of murder (and is now serving twenty-five to fifty years), and *The Jenny Jones Show* was put on trial as well.

In October 1995, Dr. William J. Bennett and Senator Joseph Lieberman (D-CT) held a press conference in which they announced that they were beginning a campaign against the production of trash TV. Their mission was twofold: to get the producers to clean up the shows and to get the viewers to stop watching them. Days later, producers and talk show hosts held a "talk summit" to determine how to be more responsible with their influential power, all the while defending their work by citing the First Amendment.[23]

The result: some of the shows since the Bennett/Lieberman press conference have gone on to "talk TV heaven," new shows have sprung up, and those that have stood the test of time have either cleaned up or gotten worse. As Jessica and I prepared this portion of the book, we talked about why teens are drawn to what she describes as "what used to be funny, but is now a circus." Here's more of what she has to say on this subject.

JESSICA'S REMARKS ON TEENS AND TELEVISION

Although I have enjoyed a variety of talk shows over the years, it wasn't until this book forced me to do so that I questioned what it was exactly that I found enter-taining about them and what made me tune in to them. That's especially true of the ones that constantly insist on pushing the envelope.

Why are America's youth so enthralled with these shows? Keep in mind that there are some popular talk shows I find completely unnec-essary and disgusting—to the point that I can't even enjoy a meal while watching them. There are others that are completely on the other end of the spectrum; these usually include stories of love, hope, joy, encourage-ment, struggle, and survival. Some, mind you. I like watching these alone so I can cry without feeling silly. Then there are the shows that are often overlooked by parents. They fall right in the middle between the other two, and we don't even notice as they con-tinue to push the lines a little further to the left. Each of these types gives a glimpse into someone's life from whatever angle has proved to bring good ratings—or is suspected to do so. In television-land, even real life bows to the rating gods, and everything is subject to the whims of the masses. And shock value sells. Of course it takes more and more these days to

The First Amendment to the United States Constitution: Congress shall make no law respecting an establishment of religion, or prohibiting the free exercise thereof; or abridging the freedom of speech, or of the press; or the right of the people peaceably to assemble, and to petition the Government for a redress of grievances.

shock us, but we sure do love it when that happens. That's what keeps our interest, and that's how the TV masters keep us from switching channels.

Herein lies, in my opinion, perhaps the scariest element: It is not that these stories actually exist, but rather that the viewers have made it so apparent to the networks that these are the kind of stories we want to watch. Why are people so drawn to this kind of programming anyway?

More to the point, I think, is the question of why are we not drawn to another type of programming? More uplifting or inspiring kind of programming? Only two words come to mind: "mindless entertainment." We seem to be searching for mindless entertainment, and "trash TV's" full and entire purpose can be summed up in those two words. It is a very simple thing, and I feel it is unnecessary to make it into too much more. The dictionary gives the definition of the word *entertain* as "to amuse or occupy agreeably."[24] Likewise for most TV viewers, these shows are mindless time consumers. Lovely concept, isn't it?

The bottom line is trash in, trash out. The latter is an inescapable rule we must face daily—no, actually moment by moment—not only deciding exactly who we will become but also choosing many of our future battles.

Of course, this is a responsibility that most children or teens do not fully understand or accept. As long as it is your responsibility to help mold the kind of character they possess, it is subsequently your job to control, to the best of your ability, what ingredients go into their making. Remember that their youth will always be their foundation.

That said, I feel that the decision of exactly which shows cross the line for you and your children should depend on the topics and content your children are ready for, and that is a decision for you, and you alone, to make. Also, making a blanket decision on any program is a mistake as the content of some programs varies drastically from episode to episode. So stay on top of your children's viewing preferences and habits. When it comes down to it, as with any other genre of media, it is your responsibility and right to decide what is and what isn't suitable intake for your "seeds."

THE DRAW OF SOAP OPERAS

In much the same way, the draw of soap operas on teen audiences has been about ratings. I remember watching *General Hospital* (1963–present) with my mother. Although the plot twists, it is typically centered around the seventh floor of General Hospital in Port Charles, New York, as well as a few outside businesses like Kelly's Diner and ELQ (the wealthy Quartermaine family's vast empire). Years later—when I was a teen—many other "soaps" were on my "must watch" list, including the new daytime drama *The Young and the Restless*, which began in 1973. In my lifetime I have viewed and/or been addicted to *All My Children, Another World, The Bold and the Beautiful, As the World Turns, Days of Our Lives, The Doctors, General Hospital, The Guiding Light, One Life to Live, Ryan's Hope,* and *The Young and the Restless.* There was a time when my entire day was scheduled around these shows; my mother-in-law and I often viewed them together, talking about the characters as though they were our best friends and neighbors.

I have since "kicked the habit" (and would have joined Soap Opera Anonymous if I thought it would have helped), but I well remember what drove me to the small screen every weekday afternoon: zany, unpredictable plotlines and interesting characters who were my contemporaries.

Soap opera producers learned fairly early on that to draw a faithful audience, they needed to keep the characters young and

... well ... restless. In the early seventies *All My Children* introduced Tara, Erica, and Phil—all young and passionate about life.
The Young and the Restless was, naturally, focused on young
Snapper, Lorie, and Jill. In the 1980s *General Hospital* jumped on
the "get 'em while they're young" bandwagon with the now
famous Luke and Laura story line.

Today, however, steamy sex has become the norm in daytime, a time when many young people will be watching. Not
may be. Will be. And the FCC has taken notice.

In early 2004 *The Guiding Light* included a segment in which
a character pulled down the underwear of her boyfriend,
exposing his bare rear end. Shortly thereafter, producer John
Conboy was "let go." A few months later, FCC commissioner
Michael J. Copps came across "steamy stuff for the middle of
the afternoon"[25] as he was channel surfing. He acted by
announcing to reporters, the day after the National Association
of Broadcasters held a summit on "responsible programming,"
that the FCC should review daytime dramas. Perhaps, he sur-
mised, they had gone too far.

Nɪɢʜᴛᴛɪᴍᴇ Sʜᴏᴡs Dᴇsɪɢɴᴇᴅ ꜰᴏʀ ᴛʜᴇ Yᴏᴜɴɢ ᴀɴᴅ ᴛʜᴇ Rᴇsᴛʟᴇss

In a *New York Times* article titled "The Ancient Days of Teenage
Drama," reporter Alessandra Stanley writes, "The high school
students of *The O.C.* do everything imaginable in their privileged
beach community in Southern California except, of course, go to
school. The show ... revels in ... all sex and no band practice."[26]
Ms. Stanley goes on to explain that in today's teenage drama (as
opposed to shows like *The Many Loves of Dobie Gillis* [1959–1963]
and *The Patty Duke Show* [1963–1966] and even more modern
shows such as the short-lived drama of 1994, *My So-Called Life*),
sex between the teen players is commonplace, though anything
but immature. Sex is very adult, only better. [27]

So then, what are our older children currently watching? Here are just a few of the popular small-screen rating busters. (Note: While these shows may or may not currently be on television—though they could be in syndication whether they are being broadcast locally or not—this lineup will give you the status to date of teen viewing preferences. It is important to note that shows aimed at teens are more often watched by preteens/tweens, while teens watch shows aimed at young adults.)

[*One Tree Hill*] is very realistic ... kids in high school may see each other naked from time to time.

—Hilarie Burton, television actress[29]

ONE TREE HILL

Synopsis: Teen friends (and enemies) attempt to survive living in Tree Hill, a town filled with secrets—most of which belong to their parents. There are love triangles, bloodline feuds, and a female lead who "seems hell-bent on partying and sleeping her way through high school."[28]

JACK AND BOBBY

Synposis: This is the story of two brothers, one who grows up to be president. No, it's not a fictional account of the Kennedy boys. This story takes place in the make-believe town of Hart, Missouri, where Jack and Bobby McAllister are being raised by their less-than-perfect mother, who is a college professor with a pot problem (and I don't mean she can't get her petunias to grow).

TRIPPING THE RIFT

Synopsis: At an online TV-show posting site, a teen wrote the following: "Has anyone seen this show on the Sci-Fi Channel? It's really really funny. Kind of dirty and crude and sexy, but funny and wild. They put a parents warning in front of it, but it's really good."

This show is a comic saga of five misfits who live, work, and play on the starship *Jupiter 42*. One look at the Web site will explain the teen's comments above.

SMALLVILLE

Synopsis: Clark Kent meets his teen years. While he is not a superhero yet, Clark struggles with a villian of another kind: adolescence.

7TH HEAVEN

Synopsis: Praised as "high-quality entertainment geared toward the entire family"[30] and named one of the best family-friendly shows by the Parents Television Council, *7th Heaven* is an ongoing saga centering on the life of the Reverend Eric Camden, his wife Annie, and their five—make that seven—children. However, as in real life, things for this TV God-believing family aren't ideal either. For example, while youngest son Simon has lost his virginity, it is noted that he practices safe sex.

THE O.C.

Synopsis: Newport Beach, in Orange County (thus the O.C.), California, is a wealthy, harbor-front community where all things appear perfect. Don't be fooled; kids live secret lives here, and so do their parents. (It should be noted that episode 12 of the 2004–2005 season ended with a lesbian kiss between two young women, Alex and Marissa.)

AMERICAN IDOL

Synopsis: *American Idol* began as *Pop Idol* in England, then crossed the shores to America, where it has truly become an international phenomenon. Each season, young singers (season four boasted 100,000 of them) try out for and then work toward being crowned the next "American Idol."

JOAN OF ARCADIA

Synopsis: The story of a typical American family ... except that the teenage daughter talks to God, who appears in a variety of ways. *Joan of Arcadia* also deals with the real-life issues of sex among teens, drunk driving, and death.

WHATEVER HAPPENED TO THE FAMILY HOUR?

During the 1970s the National Association of Broadcasters determined that 7:00 to 9:00 p.m. would be dubbed "the family hour" and that "family-friendly" shows would be aired during the two-hour time slot. For example, in 1975 the ABC, CBS, and NBC lineups for weeknights at 8:00 p.m. looked like this:

	Mon.	Tues.	Wed.	Thurs.	Fri.
ABC	*Barbary Coast*	*Happy Days*	*When Things Were Rotten*	*Barney Miller*	*Mobile One*
CBS	*Rhoda*	*Good Times*	*Tony Orlando and Dawn*	*The Waltons*	*Big Eddie*
NBC	*Invisible Man*	*Moving On*	*Little House on the Prairie*	*The Montefuscos*	*Sanford and Son*

Ten years later, the lineup was still clean, sporting dramas such as *Scarecrow and Mrs. King*, *Knight Rider*, and *Murder, She Wrote*. Comedies beginning at 8:00 p.m. were *TV's Bloopers and Practical Jokes*, *Who's the Boss*, and *The Cosby Show*.

After the use of the rating system was set firmly in place (even with some declaring its faults), the idea to go back to the "family hour" was suggested. Senator Fritz Hollings (D-SC) introduced legislation in the 103rd, 104th, and 105th Congresses to provide "safe harbor" from violent programming during a time when children would make up a larger audience.

However, parents are not so sure: only 48 percent are in favor of such regulations, while 47 percent are opposed.[31]

Why? Because many parents today are more concerned with losing their constitutional rights than their rights as parents to raise their children without exposing them early in life to adult issues early in the evening.

AFTER MIDNIGHT

I couldn't sleep. I had a million and one things to do before leaving on a weeklong speaking trip the following morning. It was late, and my husband had long since gone to bed, leaving me to my insanity of choice. In the family room, the TV continued to blink into the gray of the room, the sound muted to nothing more than a hum. I dragged the ironing board from the laundry room into the family room, determined to finish my ironing while watching an "oldie but goodie" on AMC (American Movie Classics) or TMC (Turner Movie Classics). I plugged in the iron and reached for the remote—my husband had left the television on a popular cable channel—almost in the same fluid movement. Before I could punch in the numbers for AMC, however, a new show started up ... and I froze, mouth open, jaw slack.

It was porn. Porn on a cable channel. Not necessary to pay extra for it. Not labeled an "adult channel." Porn on a cable channel! And it was just a minute after midnight.

The older your children become, the more likely their sleeping habits will change. When they are younger, you may be able to get them to bed between eight and nine o'clock. When they hit the teen years—especially the older teen years—they are just waking up at eight and nine o'clock! They become nocturnal, sleeping late on Saturdays and on summer mornings. Even during the school year, it may not be unusual for you to awaken in the middle of the night to the muffled sounds of a television in another room. Tiptoe down the hall, and you may find a room illuminated by the same shades of gray that had penetrated my family room that evening and your nearly grown child watching television.

As you step in the room to instruct your child to go to sleep, take note as to what is playing. If it's Nick at Nite (Nickelodeon), you are okay. But some of the other cable channels now play pornographic talk shows, soft-porn movies, or shows dedicated to sexual instruction. Even the commercials are pornographic to a degree. "Call me ..." a shapely and scantily clad young woman may say, "... and I'll teach you everything I know about hot love." Or there may be advertisements for products designed to produce higher levels of sexual gratification.

If you discover your child in the act of viewing inappropriate shows, that moment is not the time to discuss it. Simply turn off the set and let your son or daughter know that you'll discuss it later. (I call this "inflicting the sense of dread." It's a lot like, "Just wait till your father gets home.") When you do talk to your child about the subject, do not inflict blame or shame. Remember, your child is simply acting upon a natural curiosity—and one medium is more than happy to provide answers for youngsters' questions about sex.

TALKING TO YOUR KIDS ABOUT
SEX AND TELEVISION: EVA MARIE

According to studies done by Nielson, Nickelodeon, and the Kaiser Family Foundation, nearly 80 percent of American households have more than one television set. The average American household has the TV on approximately eight hours a day—whether it's being watched or not.

I can vouch for this fact in my own life. When I was single (a hundred years ago!), I was known to keep a television set on for "company." Today, while traveling and staying alone in hotel rooms, I continue this practice. (Funny story: while traveling in Israel, I kept my television set on all night in spite of the fact that I understood little Hebrew!)

Children ages two to eighteen watch TV more than they listen to music and certainly more than they read. The approximate number of hours per year is one thousand, or one and a half months.

In National Family Foundation President Barbara Hattemer's book *Don't Touch That Dial*[32] (cowritten with Robert Showers), there are certain messages parents cannot ignore when it comes to sexual trends in the media. Quoting Dr. Robert Kubey, she notes the following:

> Materialism. In order to be happy, one must own things.
> For everything there is a quick fix.
> Younger is better.
> Open and unfilled time is not desireable ... cannot be tolerated.
> Violence is acceptable.
> Religion is unaccepted.
> Sex is good only outside of marriage.[33]

Knowing these on-air values will help you begin to unravel part of television's not-so-hidden agenda. To grasp the extent to which your children have bought into this belief system, try the following:

Ask your children about their favorite possessions. Then ask, "If the house burned down tonight and you lost that one thing, would all your happiness and joy disappear?" Naturally, they would be sad, but what about joy? Then, share with them the words of Paul, found in Philippians 3:10. "I want to know Christ." This was Paul's "one thing," and it brought him joy.

Ask them to tell you of one time when they witnessed a "quick fix." Talk about the best things in life coming to those who wait. Share with them the story of their own birth (whether they were born into the family or adopted doesn't matter; it still takes nine long months to "grow a child") and how they were worth the wait. Remind them that even the birth of Jesus didn't come about overnight, but after thousands of years of prophecy and waiting.

Explain to them that while we are not able to do all the things we could when we were younger, growing older certainly doesn't mean growing useless. When it comes to sexuality (if appropriate for your children), share the fact that love and passion do not cease with time but become more precious. If the subject isn't age appropriate, ask them about an older person in their lives—a grandparent, aunt, uncle, and so forth. Ask why that "older person" is so dear to them.

Ask your children if they ever feel as though they are "competing" with the television for your attention. Then, set a time—whether a day, an evening, or just an hour—in which the television will not be turned on and in which you will dedicate yourself totally to them—even if you are quietly reading alongside each other.

Though violence is depicted on television as the way to solve problems, present some "what would you do?" situations for your children to decide the resolution.

Since younger children probably won't recognize the rebuke of religion as quickly as older kids will, if you see programing that slaps religion in the face, simply talk about it with your children. If the show is devoid of a religious foundation, ask your children how a relationship with God might improve the "situation." If the show gives an incorrect view of religion, speak frankly with your children, explaining the truth.

If your children seem to believe that sex is good only outside of marriage ... well, that is where your personal relationships come in. If you are married, your children should be aware that God's gift of intimacy is quite wonderful. In his article "Helping Teens Deal with Their Sexuality," youth pastor and father Chuck Gartman states that the number one guideline for teaching healthy sexuality is to "give teens loving homes where they can see a wholesome model of sexuality in their parents."[34]

If you are not married, allow me to advise you, albeit carefully. Your relationships should not be outside the will of God. You are the number one influence in your children's lives. What you do affects everything they believe. If you are living within the will of God's design for sex and intimacy but are not married, you are not without opportunity for sharing honestly with your children. We will talk about age-appropriate information later, but again, be honest. Talk to your children. It's that simple.

While we all know we can't guard the minds of our children twenty-four/seven, we can—at the very least—give them a foundation that will enable them to make wise choices when we are not there to help them in the process.

In his book *The Other Parent*, author James P. Steyer reminds parents that this is a responsibility to be taken seriously: "We can't just shut our eyes to the problem and ignore the 'other parent's' constant, cumulative influence. We have to be just as involved and aware of our kids' media use as we are of their friends, their schoolwork, and their physical and emotional well-being."[35]

Steyer's suggestions make sense and are doable. At the end of his book are detailed instructions concerning

- The establishment of good media habits early on.
- Determining to keep televisions out of your children's rooms and in a central location.
- Setting a media diet (and sticking to it).

- Teaching your kids to ask permission to watch television or use other types of media.
- Watching and listening with your kids and telling them what you like, don't like, and why.
- Setting clear rules for media consumption when your kids are away from home.
- Having pediatricians review your kids' media as part of their yearly exam.
- Teaching media literacy in school and at home.
- Reading to your children and sharing positive media experiences with them.
- Switching the dial to "off."[37]

Being a parent is the greatest responsibility we have, and God has given us his guidebook for how to be the parent he has called us to be. Problem is, most of us parents live by the rule of don't do what I do, but do what I say to do! Jesus didn't live that way and neither should we.... What example are you setting for your children?

—Scott McCurdy[36]

THINGS TO REMEMBER AS A PARENT

Once your children have heard or seen something, you can't take it back. It is now your job to explain and decipher it.

You are the gatekeeper. It is up to you to determine what your children will view and at what point you will begin to allow more explicit viewing. You can't stop the programs from being shown. You can't control the networks. But you can decide when your children will be exposed to sexual images and repartee and at what level.

To believe you can keep your children from negative impressions left by TV and other forms of media is to fool yourself.

It's worth repeating: You are the gatekeeper. If you come away with nothing else, come away with that fact.

TALKING TO YOUR KIDS ABOUT SEX
AND TELEVISION: JESSICA

Whether teens are already sexually active or not, today's youth want more information about sex-related issues. They are curious about these issues, which means that television is not just "the baby-sitter"; it is literally their teacher on whatever topics they are curious about.

According to information found at the University of Missouri-Kansas City's Web site, teenagers watch television an average of twenty-three hours each week.[38] So we know the average teen spends more time in front of the television than in the classroom. Research has proved it. But what are teenagers being taught by television? Well, for one thing, the majority of television programs (along with all other forms of media) give the impression that for sex to be romantic it should be impulsive.

If you stop and think about it, you will realize it's true. How do you think this truth could affect their decisions when it comes to their own sexual activities? What type of situations can you envision these lessons setting in motion? Really, spend some serious quiet time trying to imagine how these types of lessons could affect some of the choices your children might have to make. Does it express to you how important it is that your children be informed on even the most explicit subjects from a spiritual standpoint? When temptations are strong, you had better hope that their expectations of themselves are stronger.

WALK A MILE IN THEIR SHOES

Once you have practiced "walking in the shoes of the youth," remember that there are many similar morally devoid lessons to be learned from the tube.

It was stated previously in our book that in the year 2000, 68 percent of TV programs had sexual content. This is already an unnerving opportunity for imparting sexual morals (and lack of morals) to your children. How will these programs affect your kids, and what will you do to weaken their impact?

One of the first steps that you need to take is to do your homework; otherwise you won't know what kind of giant you and your children are up against. Do you really know what programs entertain your children? How much do you know about the lessons they teach?

It has been stated earlier that, by best estimate, parents watch TV 19 percent of the time with children under age seven and almost never with tweens and teens. Why are these numbers so low? If you listen to your children's incidental comments, they should give you a full lineup of their favorite programming. Asking them or simply tuning in with them occasionally should give you most of the rest. There are also the other ones they will not share with you ever because they fear the inevitable response. (These were also just discussed.)

By this point in your homework, you are probably beginning to wonder, "Lord, how did the jungle ever get this thick and overgrown?"

Remember, TV is not produced strictly for those with the same moral convictions as yours—or even similar convictions, for that matter. Rather, TV is produced for the "bottom line" of the financial statements of a few corporations. And the bottom line is sex sells. What's even more terrifying is the lengths that TV producers will go to provide the "shock factor" necessary for the greatest profit, all the while nudging the line a little more to the left. This is part of why "reality TV" probably doesn't remind you of any reality you know.

All the way up to the eighties, and maybe a little beyond, TV programs showed the most wholesome version of whatever situation they wanted to portray. Now, 90 percent of the time the opposite is true, and most of the time TV characters' standards probably fall well beneath your own.

Spend a little time watching some of the music videos that appeal to your kids. Music videos have additional influence because they combine both visuals and the undeniable power of music. On MTV, 75 percent of the music videos involve sexual imagery, 50 percent involve violence, and 80 percent combine the two.[39] A good place to start might be a music video countdown program, like MTV's *Total Request Live* (TRL) and BET's *106th and Park*—the two most popular that air today.

Your children exist in a reality different from yours. You have to understand that fact because when you present the issues with the programming as being a serious threat, they will probably tell you that "it's not that big of a deal" or "it's just for entertainment." This is because not much on TV can shock them. The vulgarity, sexuality, and violence of these programs show young people nothing new in light of the things they see around them every day. To them these things seem natural and insignificant. They can relate to these things through their personal experiences, and that makes them of interest to your kids. Our focus lies more on what these kinds of programs can teach us, how we relate to others, and how we can draw strength from the situations we witness and the lessons the characters are so willing to impart. And, more often than not, we watch simply to be entertained, all the while overlooking the spiritual pit of pollution we carry ourselves through. We don't consider the difficulties and moral dilemmas we are creating for ourselves and our children at a later date.

Another point to consider is how much time your children spend being entertained by television. Is it more time than they spend in school? Perhaps the ratio is less alarming than that. But even so, they may have too much free time on their hands. Even with time constraints on today's families, providing "extracurricular" activities can have a wealth of positive influence. Sports, volunteer work, youth activities, drama, part-time jobs, writing, reading, church, Bible study, or whatever fuels their interest and makes them feel good about themselves is a double-good addition to your children's lives. These types of activity can help your children feel confident in their own convictions in times of moral dilemma.

WHEN YOU TALK ...

If we insist that our children consider the TV programs they watch from a spiritual standpoint, they may try to defend them by stressing the good they teach. Although I do thank God for every seed he is able to drop into this industry, this kind of denial means that our children need our help to get back to looking through "spiritual eyes." If television is viewed strictly for entertainment purposes and not taken seriously, remind your children that "our struggle is not against flesh and blood, but against the rulers, against the authorities, against the powers of this dark world and against the spiritual forces of evil in the heavenly realms" (Eph. 6:12). Ask them what they think this verse means.

As you talk with your children, ask them to give you an example of "what goes in, comes out." Remind them that they will reap what they sow (see Gal. 6:7), which applies even to the seeds planted in their hearts and minds. Then reinforce to them (by sharing examples) that in life they will always get what they focus on, whether good or bad. Hopefully they already have the kind of spiritual background that will confirm to them the power of words and thoughts.

Ask your young men if, considering this consequence, they really think it is wise to spend their time fantasizing about and being entertained by females who do not have the morals they expect in their future wives. Ask them if they believe and can see that this kind of lustful activity will cause difficulties for them in the present and assure suffering for them in the future.

Ask your young women if they expect to become the women God could make out of them while their minds are filled with images of Jezebels and Ahabs. Now switch the questions around. Ask your son how he sees his potential, and ask your daughter how she sees her husband's. Suggest that they spend time visualizing images and detailed situations of the man or woman God has plans to mold them into and the one he has chosen to be their mate. This kind of focus and thought process will help make it so.

Be willing to give them examples of how following God's way made you happier than having your way. Ask them to give you examples of the same in their lives. Notice that in most of these examples, I use the word *ask*, and not *tell*. I believe this is the key to communicating with your children about the effects of television, but I don't suggest that you discuss all these issues in one sitting.

Explain to them that because of all these things and the temptations that do exist, it is vital that their lives be modeled after Jesus and directed by God. Try to make them understand that without him, we have no hope in this world.

Discuss the spiritual strength and discernment they have. Help make them proud of the wisdom they possess above and beyond even some of their predecessors. Show them the pride to be found in being a leader and not a follower. Continually boost their self-confidence. Tell them that, in times of great trials and confusion, they should "lean not on [their] own understanding" (Prov. 3:5), but draw their strength from the Lord. Start teaching them these things from a very young age. Last, but certainly not least, one of the most powerful things you can do with your children that will affect them is to pray. Pray with them and without them. Pray for their favorite celebrities; pray for those who influence the state of the world. Give them a sense of responsibility by asking them to pray for those who are yet to be in the spotlight but who will one day affect their younger siblings (or anyone else younger than they are). Most important, pray that the Holy Spirit will give them strength, understanding, wisdom, and guidance. And tell your kids to pray for themselves that they will allow the Holy Spirit to lead them, and that they will be willing to follow him wherever he takes them.

CHAPTER 4

That's Entertainment?

Movies, Sex, and Your Children

"But if anyone causes one of these little ones who believe in me to sin, it would be better for him to have a large millstone hung around his neck and to be drowned in the depths of the sea."

—MATTHEW 18:6

It's a Saturday. As we often do on weekends, my family is visiting my grandparents at their home located in a sleepy Southern town about an hour from our home. Lunch has been prepared and eaten; the dishes have been washed and put away. My mother is wiping down the Formica tabletop as she says, "Y'all go get ready now."

My brother and I sprint to the bathroom. We wash our hands, comb our hair, brush our teeth, and then head for the car where our parents wait with two quarters—enough to get us into the Pal Theater's Saturday afternoon matinee and buy us a small bag of popcorn and a small soft drink, which will be served in a Dixie cup with little hearts entwined about it.

It was at the Pal Theater that I learned to love the movies, where I saw Elvis singing his way through life's little ups and downs, where I learned about the Wild West while watching Spaghetti Westerns, where I sat fascinated as John Wayne proved time and again why he was, and always would be, the Duke. The Pal Theater was my time machine. It took me to places and eras I would have never been able to visit otherwise.

The Pal Theater sat in the middle of Glennville, Georgia. Our parents had only to pull up to the door, drop us off, and then—

two hours later—pick us up again. They never fretted about what we would see during the movie or the coming attractions or whether we would be exposed to subject matter we weren't quite ready for yet.

But this was another time, another place, and entertainment was—entertainment.

THE HISTORY OF SEX AND THE MOVIES

The first time an audience gathered together to watch a "moving picture" was in 1895. It's hard for us to fathom now, but this new form of entertainment wasn't for just anybody. Those who sat in the audience were essentially the same men and women who had enjoyed vaudeville and other forms of variety shows. In time, however, even the lower and working classes became patrons.

In those days, the rich and educated saw movies only as an afternoon or evening of slumming. (Really try to imagine this today, given the price of a ticket to gain entrance into a movie, not to mention the cost of popcorn and a soft drink.) As film art and craft improved, larger and more expensive movie theaters opened in the respectable entertainment centers of the cities. Filmmakers tried to appeal to a wide range of tastes and interests, much as television producers do today. In this period there was little consciousness of movies as art; they were mass entertainment. Similes linking movies with tastelessness and movie patrons with morons continually popped up in fiction and articles of the 1920s and 1930s.[1]

In the beginning, movies and sex pretty much went hand in hand, though not in the way they do today. In the 1920s the major genre emphasis was on swashbucklers, historical extravaganzas, and melodramas, although all kinds of films were being produced throughout the decade.[2] Films varied from sexy melodramas to the great comedies featuring Charlie Chaplin and

Buster Keaton. In these early days of celluloid, Hollywood cast its female actors in the roles of damsels in distress and precocious nymphets. Take, for example, Greta Garbo, whose second American film, 1926's *The Temptress*, was about a woman who brought men to ruin. That same year *Flesh and the Devil* (also starring Garbo and her off-screen lover John Gilbert), which was primarily about sex, deception, and extramarital affairs, was released.

Another 1920s sex symbol was Clara Bow, known as the "It" Girl. And if you are wondering what "It" was, it was sex appeal.

In the 1930s Marlene Dietrich—a star hailing all the way from her home in Germany—made her first two American films, in both of which she played a prostitute. It was during this decade that Mae West made her movie debut; and who—but who—exuded more sexual overtones (both in action and in word) than Mae West? To this day her one-liners continue to be sexual beacons. According to IMDB.com's feature on West, "There was no doubt she was way ahead of her time with her sexual innuendoes and how she made fun of a puritanical society."[3]

Again, there is nothing new under the sun.

It was West's 1933 films *She Done Him Wrong* (with Cary Grant) and *I'm No Angel* that resulted in the Motion Picture Production Code, or Hays Code, implemented by the Motion Picture Producers and Distributors of America (MPPDA), also known as the Hays Office. (See chapter 3, Who's Minding the Children?)

The Hays Code stated that movies were to avoid any kind of sexual promiscuity, both in word and in deed. On screen, married couples slept in separate twin beds, and the institution of marriage was viewed as sacred, not sexual. Words that today we would find tame—like "sex" and "breast"—were banned. Inclusion of the line "Frankly, my dear, I don't give a damn" (spoken by Clark Gable in *Gone with the Wind*, 1939) was highly debated. In those days, keeping content and context "clean" was of utmost importance. Today's movie moguls seek ways to get the "four-letter words" in, rather than trying to keep them out.

The Hays Code perished some thirty years after being established, ironically due to the very reasons it was implemented. America and its audiences had changed. The sixties brought a sexual revolution, both in reality and in the movies that mirrored it. Romance was out, sex was in, and film producers (as well as ordinary citizens) began to scream, "The First Amendment."

THE FIRST AMENDMENT: WHAT IT IS AND WHAT IT IS NOT

Seen a movie lately? Or should I ask, seen and *heard* a movie lately? Seeing and hearing the outright sexual content and four-letter words have become as expected as Kurt Russell in a 1960s Disney film.

Two questions come to mind here. First, why do we allow ourselves to view and listen to actors who are portraying characters whose actions and words we would never tolerate in any other settings? And second, how are the moviemakers getting away with this type of activity?

The answer to the first question varies from person to person—conscience to conscience. The answer to the second question is The First Amendment to the Constitution of the United States.

But the First Amendment, adopted in 1791, wasn't meant to give carte blanche to creative forces. It was meant to protect society, not harm it. It came from a group of people—our nation's founding fathers—who believed that people in a free society (which they had fought and died to establish) should have the right and freedom to say what they wanted to say, print what they wanted to print, and believe what they wanted to believe. These men had come from a country whose government had ruled even their relationship with God, and they wanted to assure that that level of restriction of personal freedoms would never be allowed in the new nation they were creating.

I cannot, for the life of me, believe that these men could have predicted the abuse of the First Amendment as we see it today. They would not have been able to foresee how this amendment would relate to movies, television, radio, and the Internet.

The First Amendment is tricky. While I am sure that most Americans would say they are against censorship, would they— at the same time—condone anything that approves of racism or the abuse of women and children?

Then, of course, there is the issue of art and free-flowing creativity. By calling something "art," those who would otherwise be crossing a very thin First Amendment line are able to break the rules. Take, for example, our infamous Mae West. When the Hays Code was enforced, West simply wrote the dialogue for her movies (she was more than just an actress) as to be taken "any way you like it." More recently was the case of the dancers of the Casselberry, Florida, strip club who used their First Amendment rights after an ordinance was passed keeping them from dancing nude (but instead forced them to wear G-strings and pasties). What did they do? When they realized that the ordinance had a tiny, little "artistic" loophole in it, they became creative. If their performances were considered "art," then they became bona fide artists rather than just strippers. So three dancers from the club began legally performing Shakespeare's *Macbeth* in the buff, making headlines across the country and even landing spots on news and talk shows.

The distributors of the lovely *Fly Away Home* insisted that a four-letter word be added so that the movie would avoid a G rating.

—Nell Minow, *The Movie Mom's Guide to Family Movies*[4]

THE FIRST AMENDMENT MEETS MODERN TIMES

As the founding fathers of our country couldn't have legally pre-pared for the twentieth century, so William Hays couldn't have possibly imagined that the Hays Code would eventually set America at odds with the First Amendment. The 1960s brought radical changes to America, and young people were at the fore-front of that revolution.

Hippies, also known as "flower children," were members of a youth movement that rejected the customs, traditions, and lifestyles of society, attempting to develop their own. They were "anti-establishment" and "anti-government." Anything that fit into the traditional family mold or the established way of mak-ing a living and a life was seen as passé. Most hippies came from white middle-class families and ranged in age from fifteen to twenty-five years old.[5] The hippie movement affected all areas of the media, as seen by the changes in music, clothes, television, and movies.

Though the hippie movement eventually died away in the 1970s, it made its mark in American history and in the attitudes of the people. The issues and ideas that would have had Americans up in arms in the 1950s simply no longer existed, and moviegoers wanted to see films exemplifying the times. Take, for example, 1969's *Midnight Cowboy* (MGM/UA), a movie that "broke many sexual and language taboos [and] also brought homosexuality into mainstream movies."[6]

ARE THE MOVIES COMPLETELY SINFUL?

Today, religious conservatives have made the entire entertain-ment industry an arena for battle in the wide culture wars.[7] There are religious groups and even individuals outside of those circles who believe that going to the movies is "sinful," but the purpose of this section is not to argue that point. The purpose is to help parents find a balance between a movie's negative influences and its positives, remembering that there is nothing new under the sun and that we can actually gain wisdom from the generations that have preceded us.

Let me give you an example. I have enjoyed "classic movies" my entire life (remember, I watched old Tarzan movies as a tot), and that enjoyment certainly carried over into my adult years, which includes passing the attraction to my daughter Jessica. When she was about twelve, I introduced her to the 1962 movie *That Touch of Mink* (Republic Studio), starring Doris Day as the virginal Cathy Timberlake and Cary Grant as the playboy millionaire Philip Shayne. In this comedy, Mr. Shayne gives Miss Timberlake a fetching proposal, but not one for marriage. He wants an affair, but she wants to save herself for marriage. Though at one point it looks as if Miss Timberlake will succumb to Mr. Shayne's good looks, charm, and money, in the end, she holds out, and guess what—she wins the man!

It was estimated that 70 percent of the American population in the middle of the nineteenth century thought theater attendance was sinful.

—Claudia D. Johnson in *Victorian America*[8]

In my view, this was a positive way to teach my daughter. In a friend's view, it was not. She didn't want her daughter to see even a hint of suggestion that a character might struggle with a decision in this arena. "But," I wondered, "how realistic is that viewpoint?" Logically, even at twelve, my daughter could be in similar circumstances. My role as a parent was (and is) to help my children choose between right and wrong, and I believe that lesson can be taught during the two or more hours they may spend watching a movie or video.

I also believe that, ultimately, those choices will guide us as to whether or not to even watch a particular movie or video.

Thus begins our role as parents who parent our children—using the media as a part of that parenting—and the beginning of it is knowledge.

WHAT IS THE MPAA?

The MPAA (Motion Picture Association of America) was founded in 1922 as the trade association of the American film industry. Its purpose was to assure American citizens that what they saw at the movies would be "favorable." Over the years this organization has, of course, expanded the boundaries in order to adapt to the "times."

According to the MPAA Web site (www.mpaa.org), the organization serves its members from offices in Los Angeles and Washington, D.C. On its board of directors are the chairmen and presidents of the seven major producers and distributors of motion pictures and television programs in the United States. These members include the following:

Buena Vista Pictures Distribution
(The Walt Disney Company)
Sony Pictures Entertainment Inc.
Metro-Goldwyn-Mayer Studios Inc.
Paramount Pictures Corporation
Twentieth Century Fox Film
Corporation
Universal City Studios LLLP; and
Warner Bros. Entertainment Inc.[10]

V-chips and rating systems are two more attempts to avoid responsibility on everyone's part—the producers, the advertisers and the television audience.

—Robert P. Lockwood, *Our Sunday Visitor*[9]

The conflict of interest is obvious: The MPAA voting members would never do anything to hurt the ratings of their own movies. So how then did this voluntary rating code even begin?

In 1966, after movies won free-speech protection, the Hays

Code was officially dropped. In 1968 a voluntary, industry-wide system, called the Motion Picture Code and Rating Program, replaced it.

In the beginning there were four general ratings:

G: General Audiences. All ages admitted.

PG: Parental Guidance Suggested.

R: Restricted Audience. (Originally referred to as "M" for mature audiences.) No one under the age of seventeen admitted unless accompanied by an adult.

X: No one under seventeen admitted.

Since that time, we have seen a few other letters of the alphabet added.

PG-13: Parental Guidance Suggested. Some material may be inappropriate for children under the age of thirteen.

NC-17: Basically the same as "X."

NR: Not Rated. This label is placed on movies that were made before the rating code was established or if, at the time of the preview, a code had yet to be assigned.

Does this system work? In my opinion, and in the opinion of every authoritative figure to whom I have spoken or whose work I have read and studied, hardly. Talk to any given number of parents, open the discussion to the rating system, and you will see eyes rolling. Some movies with a PG rating you can take your child to, and some you can't. Some PG-13s should be rated R. Some Rs should be rated PG-13. Recently, as I sat chatting with a group of Christian teens, I was surprised to hear them say that getting into an R-rated movie was fairly easy—unless, that is, the film was Mel Gibson's 2004 epic, *The Passion of the Christ*, which was rated R for scenes of graphic violence.

Go figure.

ALPHABET SOUP (THE PROBLEM WITH THE ABC SYSTEM)

On a recent Sunday afternoon, Jessica and I decided we wanted to see a movie, one that would appeal to both of us. We jumped in my car and headed for a shopping mall that boasted a theater. Standing before the marquee lineup, we agreed on the summer comedy *Raising Helen*.

Raising Helen (Buena Vista, 2004) is a delightful movie about a young, career-driven, sex-in-the-city kind of woman who finds herself raising her nieces and nephew after the tragic death of their parents. Forced to make decisions she had never anticipated, she moves herself and her new family to Queens, enrolls them in a private Lutheran school, and becomes a receptionist in a "previously owned" car dealership. The movie is cute and funny and is deemed "family oriented." However, parents should note that it is rated PG-13 for sexual content between both teens and adults, as well as for language.

While I discussed this film with my husband the following day, he noted that we—as a family and with our granddaughter—had watched *Shrek* (DreamWorks, 2001) for the one-hundredth time earlier that weekend. Though animated and considered a fairy tale, the movie is rated PG for language and crude humor. My husband also pointed out the sexual humor that is typically recognized only by adults but is—nonetheless—there.

In his book *Hollywood vs. America*, film critic Michael Medved reveals a problem with the "alphabet system." According to his findings, in 1991 (which was quite a few years ago!) the "average R-rated movie contain[ed] twenty-two F-words, fourteen S-words, and five A-words." Of course, you might say, that's an R-rated movie. But notice the rest of what Medved writes:

> Far more surprising is the ubiquity of harsh language
> in films deemed more appropriate for youthful audiences
> … 39 percent of the 1991 PG-13 films used the F-word, 66

percent used the A-word, and an amazing 73 percent used the S-word! Even among PG movies—films to which parents eagerly bring their six- and seven-year-old children—58 percent use the A-word, and 46 percent use the S-word. Insisting on this sort of language in so many films for kids is not only unnecessary; it is insane.[11]

The rating system is based on a narrow definition of "objectionable material" (one that constantly changes) and is not based on the age or maturity of your children. How are you as a parent, then, to know exactly what the letters mean when it comes to your little ones?

Allow us to break it down for you just a bit.

RATED G

Within the context of G-rated movies should be nothing— absolutely nothing—that would raise so much as a feather on an eyebrow. No nudity, no sex or sexual context, no foul language, and no violence. As a parent, you are safe here, and so are your children.

The problem in years past with G-rated films is that most people see them as being only for ages six and under, and tweens and teens would rather "die" than be caught watching something rated G. I say "years past" because in the preceding decade movies such as *Toy Story*, *The Lion King*, *A Bug's Life*, and *Finding Nemo* managed to draw audiences of every age.

Still, typically, the G rating doesn't draw tweens and teens to fill the theater seats. So what's a studio to do? Throw in brief nudity with a touch of violence or horror, and—bingo!—a PG rating.

RATED PG

A PG rating is given to those movies containing themes parents may consider unsuitable for their younger children. Yes, in these films you will find some violence and/or obscenity, though certainly less offensive than what you will find in a PG-13, R, or

NC-17 movie. No, these are not the movies containing drug use, but, yes, you may find sexual themes, brief nudity, and/or sensuality. In his book *The Media-Wise Family*, Dr. Ted Bachr states that these are the films "parents are encouraged to find out more about ... before letting children see [them]."[12]

RATED PG-13

The PG-13 guideline was established after a string of films in the 1980s, which displayed too much violence and yet were aimed at youth culture, brought religious and consumer groups together, expressing the potential harm to a young person who was not yet mature enough for such viewing. Years ago, if moviemakers wanted to raise the stakes just a bit higher and go for a PG-13 rating, they found it necessary to throw in the F-word—just once, and it couldn't refer to the sexual act. This is no longer the case. The MPAA does not have a sliding scale or a chart for rating movies that states, "X number of F-words means an automatic R rating." That would be censorship, and we have already talked about that subject. Today, the PG-13 rating exists to say that some material may be unsuitable for children younger than thirteen. But, again, quoting Dr. Baehr, "specific criteria for this rating category are ill-defined."[13]

You may wonder why movie distributors would want to take a perfectly good family film and mess with it just enough to raise the rating. I have two well-grounded theories.

The first is the one your mother always told you about: a lack of imagination.[14] My mother used to say that using four-letter words was an ignorant man's way of using the English language. The older I get, the more I have to agree with her. When we are unable to express ourselves intelligently, we resort to crude (ignorant) language.

The second theory is rather obvious: an abundance of greed. In other words, it is "an effort to raise the bounty." It's kind of like the theme of the *Field of Dreams:* "If you build it, they will come." There is the belief (and I have heard it argued on both sides) that tweens and teens are more apt to want to see a movie rated "inappropriate" than one rated "appropriate"—which is based on the age-old desire to be seen as adults as quickly as they can!—and distributors believe that with their income now being higher than at any other time in history, tweens and teens will flock to see anything even slightly risqué.

RATED R

Movies are typically rated R because of violence, sexual situations and nudity, and drug use. Sadly, the broad spectrum of what constitutes an R-rated movie leaves parents in the dark when it comes to content. Dr. Ted Baehr, in an article for *Movieguide,* cites *Almost Famous* (DreamWorks, 2000) as a case in point. Rated R for language, drug content, and brief nudity, it is about a fifteen-year-old but not for fifteen-year-olds.

According to the MPAA guidelines, children under the age of seventeen are "restricted" from entering theaters showing R-rated films unless they are with a parent or an adult guardian. How, exactly, theater owners and ticket counter clerks are to know a child's parent from Mrs. Robinson (of *The Graduate* fame) is never explained.

Movies rated R can carry a boatload of language. Take for example, 1997's *Good Will Hunting* (Miramax, 1997), cowritten by then up-and-coming actors Matt Damon and Ben Affleck. A look at the transcript of the movie reveals use of the F-word in various forms 139 times, while the original script used it "only" 92 times. However, film critics praised the work, which was nominated for an Academy Award, and Damon and Affleck went on to win the Oscar for Best Original Screenplay.

Rated NC-17

Originally the "X" in the rating system, NC-17 means that no children under the age of seventeen can be admitted whether they are accompanied by an adult or not. Movies rated NC-17 may contain strong violence, sex, aberrational behavior, drug use, and other elements parents don't want their children to view.[15] The problem with changing the X to NC-17 is that it seems friendlier somehow. Parents certainly know not to allow their children to see a movie rated X. The very stance of the letter says, "do not enter." But NC-17 seems to offer an option.

As a parent you should note that NC-17, R, PG-13, and PG are voluntary ratings. Whether or not your children are able to enter the theater is up to the person behind the counter, and, if posted, the individual standing at the doorway to the individual movies. What will happen if your children do enter one of these restricted movies? Nothing. Why? Because it is not illegal to sell a movie ticket to a minor.

The New R-card

The R-card is like a driver's license or a credit card in size and shape and is something parents purchase for their children, giving them permission to enter R-rated films without the presence of an adult. It is fairly easy to see the problem or flaw within the R-card system: R-rated movies, as previously stated, run a wide gamut.

Though there is no age limit—theoretically anyone can purchase an R-card for an underage child—parents must be the ones to purchase it from theaters. And parents have the right, certainly, to hold on to the card between shows. Parents still have the right to (at least verbally) determine which shows their children can and cannot walk into. Then, ultimately, it is up to the children to walk into the purchased movie.

WHY DO CHILDREN AND TEENS FLOCK TO THE MOVIES?

I have a friend who enjoys a weekly excursion to the movies. Every week. Sometimes more than once a week. And, sometimes, she sees the same movie more than once, more than twice even. I can't imagine what this regular movie habit does to her pocketbook, and so I commented one afternoon about the cost efficiency of waiting for the films to come out on videocassette, DVD, or Pay Per View. She immediately came back with, "Some movies are just meant for the big screen."

According to a Gallup poll conducted in early 2003, 40 percent of teens say there is too much sex in movies.[16]

I agreed, and she went on to say, "Since I was a child, I've loved going to the movies. But not just to see the movie itself. I want the entire experience. I want the popcorn and the drink as well."

I have said that I have always enjoyed walking out of the dark theater into the light of day and then having to blink a few times before reality returns. And, as I mentioned a few pages ago, going to the movies has been a part of my life as far back as I can remember, whether it was at the Pal Theater (which was indoors) or at my hometown's local drive-in, where car windows were often known for getting steamy and watching the movies was not always the central focus of the ticketbuyers.

Recently, while talking with Ken Wales, president of Ken Wales Productions, I asked, "Why has going to the movies always been such a hot ticket when it comes to dating?"

"Because it's cheap entertainment," he quipped.

Kids today don't have to fork out nearly ten dollars per person to see a movie; nearly every American home sports a TV and a VCR and/or DVD player. Many own more than one. I personally know of a number of homes with a TV and VCR/DVD player in nearly every room.

Even with the price of tickets today, going to the movies—as in days past—is the thing to do as a child, a tween, and especially as a teen with a dating budget. (According to Teenage Research Unlimited,[17] 91 percent of teens consider going to the movies as the number one "in thing" to do.) But "dinner and a movie" wasn't always the path a couple took in order to get to know one another better and to explore the possibilities.

There was a time, oh, about a hundred years or so ago, when a young man (known as a "suitor") "called on" a young woman by knocking on her front door and then sitting with her and her family in the parlor. Courting candles, lit by the parents of the young lady, were for letting the young man know when it was time to go home. When the flame had burned the wick to a nub … well, that was his cue to leave.

During the Depression, when large families often shared small living spaces, dating outside the house became both preferred and acceptable. Life was difficult enough, and finding an escape via "amusements" helped ease the agony of reality.

But entertainment cost money. Because single women who were unemployed made no money and those who were employed made significantly less than their male counterparts, it was therefore the man who paid for the date. With the cheap price of a movie ticket, taking a girl to a show was the logical thing to do. It provided a safe environment and a getaway from the harsh realities of life. It also allowed, however, for more private time between a guy and his girl.

It was during the post–World War II era that a change in the movie audience took place, specifically from the "family" market to the "thirty and under" market. The transition crossed the boundaries of media, taking root in music as well as movies. Added to this change was the influx of a new breed of Americans: teenagers, whose very presence seemed to dominate the 1950s.

As the relative calm of the 1950s eased into what would become the increasing turbulence of the 1960s, sixteen- to twenty-four-year-olds became the primary moviegoers. As a result, by the late sixties, and in the interest of expanding profits, the entertainment industry focused itself on youth culture and continued to do so for the next twenty years. The entertainment media and popular cultural industries knew beyond all doubt that they were "capable of selling fashions, selling products and communicating ideas."[19] It only made sense, then, to make movies for teens, about teens, and with products sellable to teens.

Did you know the word *teenager* was first used in 1921 ... that the expected number of teens is expected to be at 33.5 million by the year 2010, and that their rate of growth far outpaces the rest of the population?[18]

In a recent conversation with actor and movie stuntman James Sang Li,[20] I asked, "Why do movie producers put so much time and effort into making movies that appeal to young people, despite the fact they (the movies) have no artistic value?"

He answered, "Bottom line ... they're easy to produce, and they make money. Sex, drugs, and rock and roll are easy subjects to film because they are alluring to audiences and easy to sell. People come and see these types of films because Hollywood over time has made a machine that fuels curiosity in these subjects. Movies about stand-up guys, brave warriors, people that risked their lives for 'the cause'—Martin Luther and Jesus, for example—are difficult to make. They tend to be very risky, expensive, and controversial."[21]

THE TWEEN-TEEN MOVIE SENSATION

The large screen's competition with the small screen means creating steamier, sexier scenes in order to entice patrons to leave the comfort of their living rooms, lay down their money, and then pay a small fortune for the same snacks they could get at home for small change. This is, of course, especially true for young audiences. Youth-oriented films aim at the main area of adolescents' lives at the highest rank of turmoil: their sexuality.

For the most part, when your children get old enough to enter a theater without you is when both of you are most vulnerable. It is at this point that everything you have taught them will be put into practice. You hope that the foundations you have laid in their early years by watching cartoons and family flicks with them will last a lifetime.

The making of "teen movies" began in the 1950s and has grown steadily stronger with each generation because moviemakers have the desire to express the joys and angst of the generation, especially its youth culture. They define fashion and fads (the 1950s were as much about leather jackets and rock and roll as they were about bomb shelters and stay-at-home moms) while creating the idols our children believe they want to imitate. The 1950s gave the teen world a plethora of idols to choose from— from James Dean to Sandra Dee—proving that it wasn't so much about the plotline of the movie as much as who held the starring role. Can you imagine *A Streetcar Named Desire* (1951) without Marlon Brando or *A Summer Place* (1959) without Troy Donahue?

In the 1950s Hollywood began to produce what was called the JD (juvenile delinquent) films such as *Blackboard Jungle* (1955) and *High School Confidential* (1958), which was one of the first movies to deal with teens and drugs.

The 1960s produced its fair share of "beach movies" starring Frankie Avalon and Annette Funicello (with movie tag lines like "It's where the girls are BARE-ing, the guys are DARE-ing, and the surf's RARE-ing to GO-GO-GO"), while other social ways of life were explored in movies like *To Sir, with Love* (1967) and *The Graduate* (1967).

The 1970s teen movies had an "against the rules" feel to them. In *Love Story* (1970), rich boy Oliver Barrett IV (Ryan O'Neal) defied his parents to marry poor girl Jenny Cavalleri (Ali MacGraw). Though technically an "adult movie" (rated PG), every moviegoer in Movie-land flocked to stand in line outside theaters. (I was only thirteen at the time, and though that was quite a few years ago, I remember the anticipation well!) While *Animal House* (1978) expressed bedlam in college, *American Graffiti* (1973) expressed the joys and agonies of seniors graduating from high school in the

"Mrs. Robinson, you are trying to seduce me.... We could do something else, Mrs. Robinson. We could go to a movie."

—Dustin Hoffman to Anne Bancroft in *The Graduate*[22]

early 1960s (the film's poster asked, "Where were you in '62?"). John Travolta made his big-screen mark with two late seventies films, one of which (*Saturday Night Fever*, 1977) set the entire disco craze in motion.

The 1980s was the decade of the teen movies, introducing the "brat pack" (Emilio Estevez, Anthony Michael Hall, Rob Lowe, Andrew McCarthy, Demi Moore, Judd Nelson, Molly Ringwald, and Ally Sheedy) and an underwear-and-oxford clad young Tom Cruise dancing to Bob Seger's "Old Time Rock 'n' Roll" in *Risky Business* (1983), the story of a seventeen-year-old whose world collapses when he gets hooked up with a call girl. Other movies that made their mark on youth culture during the eighties were *Sixteen Candles, Pretty in Pink, The Breakfast Club, Ferris Bueller's Day Off, Some Kind of Wonderful, Fast Times at Ridgemont High, The Karate Kid*, and, of course, *Back to the Future*.

Teen movies had taken on a whole new look.

Enter the nineties.

Clueless (1995, tag line: "Sex, clothes, popularity ... whatever") was rated PG-13 for sex-related dialogue and some teen use of alcohol and drugs. *American Pie* (1999, tag line: "There's something about your first piece") was rated R for strong sexuality, crude sexual dialogue, language, and drinking, all involving teens. Though *Trojan War* (1997) deals with a teen male who is about to "get lucky" when he discovers he doesn't have a condom, it is rated PG-13.

And then the year 2000 brought the teen movies of the next millennium, starting with the popular teen flick *Bring It On*, rated PG-13 for sex-related material and language.

RECENTLY IN A THEATER NEAR YOU

To keep you, as a parent, up to date on the move of teen movies—whether they did well at the box office or not—here is a list of just a few of the teen movies for 2000–2004 (current) and their ratings (please note that these movies are for "teens") from www.hollywoodteenmovies.com and their MPAA ratings www.according to IMDB.com.

MOVIES WITH TWEEN APPEAL AND PRE-TWEEN APPEAL

Josie and the Pussycats—Rated PG for sensuality and language

Scooby-Doo—Rated PG for some crude humor, language, and scary action

The Lizzie McGuire Movie—Rated PG for mild thematic elements

Freaky Friday—Rated PG for mild thematic elements and some language

The Princess Diaries—Rated G

Spider-Man—Rated PG-13 for stylized violence and action

Confessions of a Teenage Drama Queen—Rated PG for mild thematic elements and brief language

Sleepover—Rated PG for thematic elements involving teen dating, some sensuality and language

MOVIES WITH TEEN APPEAL

Bring It On—Rated PG-13 for sex-related material and language

Whatever It Takes—Rated PG-13 for thematic elements, sexual material, and language

Almost Famous—Rated R for language, drug content, and brief nudity

40 Days and 40 Nights—Rated R for strong sexual content, nudity, and language

Dude, Where's My Car?—Rated PG-13 for language and some sex- and drug-related humor

American Pie 2—Rated R for strong sexual content, crude humor, language, and drinking

Not Another Teen Movie—Rated R for strong, crude sexual content and humor, language, and some drug content

For years, research has shown that it is children who go to R-rated movies (80 percent of the audience for R-rated movies are youth—60 percent under seventeen years old), while more mature moviegoers prefer PG and G fare.

—Dr. Ted Baehr[23]

Crazy/Beautiful—Rated PG-13 for mature thematic material involving teens, drug/alcohol content, sexuality, and language

A Walk to Remember—Rated PG for thematic elements, language, and some sensual material

Bend It Like Beckham—Rated PG-13 for language and sexual content

Save the Last Dance—Rated PG-13 for violence, sexual content, language, and brief drug references

Legally Blonde—Rated PG-13 for language and sexual references

Scary Movie 3—Rated PG-13 for pervasive crude and sexual humor, language, comic violence, and drug references[24]

The Girl Next Door—Rated R for strong sexual content, language, and some drug/alcohol use

Mean Girls—Rated PG-13 for sexual content, language, and some teen partying

Dodgeball—Rated PG-13 for rude and sexual humor and language[25]

8 Mile—Rated R for strong language, sexuality, some violence, and drug use

USING THE RATING SYSTEM AS A STARTING POINT

In his book *The Media-Wise Family,* Dr. Ted Baehr begins chapter 6 (The Ratings Game) with the following statement:

> Developing discernment requires more than realizing there is a problem, that the mass media influence behavior, or even understanding why people are influenced by the mass media. It also requires understanding in advance what the particular entertainment medium is offering and having systems in place to help you make the right choices.[26]

A recent conversation with actor Bruce Marchiano (best known for his role as Jesus in Reghardt van den Bergh's *The Gospel of Matthew)* led me to a sobering conclusion: parents—not media—are ultimately responsible for raising their children. Producers, directors, and movie distributors are not worried about the effects of their work on your children. Quite frankly, they know the power and influence they wield over youngsters, and they simply don't care that it might have a negative influence on them. Your children are not their problem. You and I have been given the most prized of possessions, our children, and how we prepare them for the world is not only our responsibility, but also it is of the utmost importance.

So what should we do? Build a bomb shelter, stock it with plenty of canned goods and toilet paper, and then go underground to raise our kids? Or should we build little men and women of God who, once they are on the battlefield, are ready for any of the "fiery darts" the Enemy may throw their way? (See Eph. 6:16 KJV). If you can take a real look at the world as it exists for you and then as it exists for your children every day and still not believe that your children are in a perilous, daily struggle, then I suggest you get your glasses checked. I don't mean that disrespectfully, but honestly and with sincerity. It doesn't matter who you are or who your children are, expect—know beyond a shadow of a doubt—that they are dealing with temptations and a reality unlike anything you could imagine for them. If you can grasp even a small part of this concept, then you will start to see the importance of your support during these times in your children's lives.

Every morning, even before they leave your home, thanks to the media, your children are literally going off to battle. Ask yourself this question: "Who is supplying their weaponry?" Don't think for one second that the old weapons they received in Sunday school aren't rusty, broken, or even obsolete by now, as far as your children are concerned.

Most parents are great at talking to their kids about drugs, sex, and so forth when they are young, when they listen with open minds and hearts to everything their parents say. Young kids will even agree with their parents, a situation that often changes later on.

But why aren't parents as quick to have these kinds of conversations with their children when they are older and have developed their own opinions? This is when they need application! Do you really think that day after day while these temptations are being loaded onto your children, all those lessons from Sunday school and Bible study with Mom and Dad are the first things that pop into their minds as a means to resist evil? Even if they do, do you think that the memory is strong enough to overcome all these pressures?

About two years ago, I began my real estate sales career. In much of my training and firsthand experience, I realized that when talking to a married couple as potential buyers, one is usually more receptive than the other. I also learned that it is human nature to talk to the most receptive; it's just more comfortable. I

also learned that, unfortunately, no matter how good a relationship you have with one spouse, and no matter how convincing
your presentation may be, it is almost invariable that the spouse
you ignore, for reasons of comfort, will be the one to convince
the other to say no. One of the biggest obstacles and hardest lessons in the business is to learn to warm up to that less-than-
receptive party and spend at least an equal amount of time with
both of them. This is the only way you will ever sell to them.

The same is true with your children. A lot of parents stop
"selling" to their children as soon as it starts to get uncomfortable, which (surprise, surprise) is exactly when children need
their parents most. When they are children, they believe nearly
anything their parents tell them. You are the parent, and to your
young children that makes you a superhero! But as they grow
older and begin to deal with the truths of the world, they
become less and less convinced of your superhuman powers
and wisdom. They need to be sold, and you are the sales executive. Their resistance is almost a measure of exactly how much
they do need you.

So why run away from this challenge? Let me assure you that
when you do, you are running away from your children and
leaving them alone in the middle of a battle from which they cannot run away. Why not, instead, run to their side, take up a
sword, and join them in the fight?

There is a difference, you know, in the role of parents and the
role of Hollywood in this whole thing. I can't stress this enough:
Hollywood's producers, directors, and so forth, as a whole don't
care about your specific children, nor are they responsible for
how they are raised.

You are. And, if you're like me most of the time, all the
brouhaha about movies can be quite confusing.

In a 1999 article for USA Today, Michael Medved clearly states
that the important people in Hollywood are more interested in

getting the little gold statue known as Oscar than being associated with a blockbuster in terms of money. "Commercial success may mean money," Medved states, "[but] victory at the Academy Awards ... signifies the respect of peers."[27]

THE ROLE OF THE PARENT VERSUS THE ROLE OF HOLLYWOOD

Then how can you as a parent know what is in the movies your children wish to see? First, you have to assume that your children will be honest about the movies they attend. I hate to say, "Be a one-person gestapo," but you may want to note here that when movie tickets are purchased, the title of the movie is on the stub. You shouldn't necessarily trust that just because your children said they went to see a PG-rated film that they didn't go see one rated R. However, there are ways around this predicament. As you will read later in the "Christian Teens at the Round Table" section in the back of this book, tickets for *Winnie the Pooh* (rated G) showing in theater 3 (for example) can be purchased at the ticket counter, but that doesn't mean your children won't walk into theater 7 where *The Girl Next Door* (rated R) is playing.

Still, there are places to go for help. For example, Ted Baehr's Web site, Movieguide.org, provides detailed reports on movies using a system that ranges from Exemplary to Abhorrent (with Moral, Good, Wholesome, Caution, Extreme Caution, and Excessive in between) as they rate films in moral acceptability. The site also includes "News and Notes" and articles by Dr. Baehr, offering a full scope of information to keep parents informed and up to date.

Crosswalk.com's Fun Channel features information on select, recently released movies. Entertainment critic Annabelle Robertson reviews seven movies each month, giving details about each film (such as its MPAA rating, director, actors, and so forth), followed by an easy-to-read parent information guide that ends with a "dot system" (· = Mild / ·· = Average / ··· = Heavy / ···· = Extreme) to help parents determine which movies are best for their children.

Focus on the Family's *Plugged In* Online details movies by breaking down their positive elements versus their negative elements, such as sex, violence, drug and alcohol content, and crude or profane language, and at the end of the review (which runs about 1,200 to 1,500 parent-friendly words) is the critic's conclusion.

> Even a movie with some objectionable material can have some value if it prompts a discussion about objectionable behavior [with your children] … it gives you a chance to talk about values without sounding as though you are preaching to them.
>
> —Nell Minow,
> *The Movie Mom's Guide to Family Movies*[28]

IMDB.com (Internet Movie Database), though not a faith-based site, will keep you up to date on all the movies that are or were showing (and even those currently in production and preproduction). IMDB.com also contains Web pages and information about current and past television shows.

TEACHABLE MOMENTS

In her book *The Movie Mom's Guide to Family Movies*, Nell Minow (who, coincidentally, is the daughter of Newton Minow, former chairman of the FCC) gives both encouragement and warnings to parents when it comes to viewing movies with their children. "Nowhere is safe," she writes. "I took my kids to see a G-rated movie and sat through a coming attraction in which a woman said to a man, 'I'm going to give you lots of sex.'"[29]

These moments *can*, however, be teaching tools if you seize them as opportunities to talk with your children rather than hoping they didn't happen to hear or catch the offense. Believe me, they heard it. "Little pitchers have big ears," my mother always said—and she was right!

Parents will do well if they remember that movies show us the modern equivalent of parables or *Aesop's Fables.* Characters confront moral dilemmas; they evaluate risk, establish priorities, adapt to change, learn important lessons, overcome loss and fear, grapple with responsibility, face consequences, solve problems, and find redemption; and in doing so, they teach children how to do those things as well.[30] In other words, movies can be excellent teaching tools and can lend themselves to teachable moments with children. Remember, however, that the bottom line is how these things are done. Not all movies show positive choices.

For example, the movie *Thirteen* (Twentieth Century Fox, 2003) is a story about thirteen-year-old Tracy Freeland, who, as her mother puts it, was "playing with Barbie dolls before she met Evie," the bad influence in Tracy's life. Though the movie is rated R for drug use, self-destructive violence, language, and sexuality—all involving young teens—and should not be viewed by children, the very title and advertisements for the movie made it a draw for young people.

More than any other age-group of children, teens and tweens look to the media or other outside sources to stretch their boundaries of behavior. For example, your children may—like you—believe that even the lightest form of swearing is wrong. A trip to a movie, a few dozen swear words spoken by cool teen characters, and your children may suddenly have a new vocabulary. Chances are, as a parent, you will not even have seen this coming, nor will you have seen this movie, as teens and tweens tend not to go to films with their parents but rather with their peers. (Yes, the same children who loved to go to a movie with you in their early years will opt, as they get older, to go with their friends.) Or they may have caught an hour or more of an R-rated video playing on the TV monitor while perusing the shelves at the local video store. And finally, they may be visiting the home of a friend whose parents don't have the same code of ethics as you.

MORE TEACHABLE MOMENTS

Let's begin with the aforementioned movie, *Thirteen*. I recently asked author, speaker, and teen expert Jessica Weiner[31] what teachable moments might be found in a movie as disturbing as this one. "Ask them to tell you how they felt when they saw the girl played by Evan Rachel Wood [Tracy] getting deeper and deeper into drugs and sex," she answered. "How did they feel when her mom didn't help her? How did they feel when the other girl manipulated her and lied to her? All of these will get them talking on the point of the movie but will allow them to generalize and express their feelings safely."

According to Ms. Weiner, movies can create steps you can take to start dialogue with your children early on and often. Use the plot points to help them identify their emotions and feelings. Open-ended questions like "So what did you think?" should be replaced with questions that require specific answers. For example, "What did you think when thus and such happened?"

"Remember," Ms. Weiner says, "it won't be a Hallmark moment but rather a series of moments that will lead up to the trust and respect our children need from us."

CHAPTER 5

American Girl to CosmoGIRL!, Boy's Life to Playboy

Magazines, Sex, and Your Children

Treat younger men as brothers ... and younger women as sisters, with absolute purity.

—1 TIMOTHY 5:1–2

It was always in the height of excitement that I waited for my *American Girl* magazines to come in the mail. The covers were slick, and the pages were filled with stories, poetry, and photos of girls who were like me: young and American. I read every line, studied each photograph, and memorized some of the poetry.

I distinctly recall as a teenager (years following my days of *American Girl* reading) taking a trip to the doctor's office. Not wanting to go alone, I called my good friend Beverly and asked if she would like to tag along. "Sure," she said, so I drove over to pick her up.

I pulled into her driveway in my '65 Mustang (fast becoming a classic) and honked the horn. Within moments, she bounded down the front porch steps. She was, as always, cute as a bug.

Beverly was fashion's princess, and it was no wonder. In her clutches, as she slipped onto the red vinyl upholstery of the passenger's seat, was her latest copy of *Glamour*. Or maybe it was *Vogue*. Whatever it was, the pages—slick and shiny like my old *American Girl*—were filled with ads for cosmetics and clothes. For the next hour or so, as we waited patiently (pardon the pun) in the doctor's waiting area for my name to be called, we turned each page slowly, sniffing the perfume ads, examining and discussing the latest in fashion, makeup (Bonne Bell was huge that year), and hair care.

But not once do I remember ever reading anything—in teen or fashion magazines—telling me which sexual positions were best, or whether or not I was still a virgin, or if I preferred to have lesbian sex versus heterosexual sex. Not once was I given the latest information on postpartum depression or the best time, astrologically, to have sex with my boyfriend. And not once was I entertained by stories about living naked or whether or not the size of a man's penis—were he to declare it on a tee-shirt—would matter to "gals on the prowl."

Today's girls (and boys), however, are facing a whole new sphere of influence when it comes to magazines.

Today's Teen Magazines

Open any magazine, especially those designed for girls, and really pay attention. Before one word of an article is printed, before the table of contents or the letter from the editor, you will find full-color advertisements. They are glossy. They are enticing. And they are sexy. They are also age deceptive. Have a short talk with teens, and you will quickly discover that teen magazines are for tweens, and young adult magazines are for teens.

According to a report published by MediaPost's *Media Daily News* dated Tuesday, June 22, 2004, "the big a-ha ... uncovered [in a Magazine Publishers Association survey] is that teens *are* reading magazines" (emphasis mine).[1] The report also shows that, to be specific, eight out of ten teens read magazines—not only teen-related but adult-themed magazines as well. "They read upward as well," says Harlan Schwarz.[2] In a similar report, Michael Shields notes, "A fourteen-year-old boy might be reading *Boy's Life*, and he might be reading *Blender* and *Maxim* as well."[3]

THE MERCHANTS OF COOL

Why are magazines so popular, especially among our youth?

With older teens (sixteen to seventeen years of age) having nearly $4,500 in annual discretionary income, they are able to purchase things for themselves such as clothes, DVDs, CDs, cosmetics, and so forth.[5] And, according to reports, they trust what they read in magazines more than any other form of media. If the ad appeals to their eye, they will purchase the product. If the articles say it's true, they will believe it.

There are two problems here:

One: The trends keep changing.

How do marketers know what will or will not appeal to the young eye? Answer: groups (known as the Merchants of Cool) such as Look-Look, a research company specializing in youth culture. By staying in the middle of young people, by asking all the right questions, and being in all the right places, research companies such as Look-Look know what (and who) kids will respond to as being "cool."

Cool sells. So when young people are looking at an ad in a magazine, the marketers have done their homework and are banking on what will be seen as being the hottest item to fly off the shelves.

Allow me to give you an example of a recent fragrance ad that not only caught my eye, but got my attention as well. It is a black-and-white shot of two young people—one male, one female. She is wearing her underwear; he is naked from the waist up. They

When they are 12 they read *Seventeen.* *Seventeen* is hampered by their name. Teens are very label-conscious. They don't want to be called teens, and don't want to be called girls. All [teen magazines] skew toward 15-year-olds. *CosmoGIRL!, Teen People* are all aiming younger. They are all giggly.

—Linda Fears, editor-in-chief, *YM (Your Magazine)*[4]

are cuddling on a bed—hair tousled—she is hugging a couple of pillows, his hand is on her waist, and his lips are close to her shoulder. The caption reads "scent to bed."

The name of the fragrance? fcuk.

Yes, you read that correctly.

FCUK stands for French Connection United Kingdom, but what the marketers have done is take two elements within youth culture (the idea that sex is playful and fun, and what is probably the most popular slang word among youth today) and used them to appeal to the masses.

Two: Not everything young people see or read in a magazine is true.

Let me provide you a few examples of truth versus myth to share with your tweens or teens.

- *YM* (Your Magazine) cannot fix everything in your life that "sucks."[6]
- Just because you wear a bathing suit ordered from Victoria's Secret does not mean you will look like a Victoria's Secret model.
- Though Britney and Madonna were named "best friends" and "spiritually bonded" by the weekly *Us* magazine[7] after their onstage kiss (during the 2003 MTV Video Music Awards show), same-sex kissing does not best friends make.
- Every lyric Beyoncé Knowles has ever written has not come from the Lord.
- Nudity is not fashion.
- Virginity is sacred.

DO YOU SEE WHAT I SEE?

Notably one of the most popular magazines for women of all time, *Cosmopolitan* made headlines when it spun off with

CosmoGIRL! But how different is one from the other? Let's look.

Cosmopolitan

Recent issues of *Cosmo*, as it is typically called, have featured articles such as "What Sex Feels Like for a Guy," "Little Words and Gestures Men Crave," "His Hidden Hot Spots," "Kama Sutra Special,"[8] "Men Unzipped," "Celeb Sex-capades," "3 Things Guys Crave in Bed," and "Your Hands-on Guide to Solo Sex."

CosmoGIRL!

While the teen version of the ever-popular *Cosmo* doesn't feature how-to articles, it does talk about boy toys. In fact, between the articles about celebs, fashion tips, and exercise hints, *CosmoGIRL!* features its own centerfold of "male eye candy" wearing nothing but a towel ... or a surfboard ... or whatever.

Suffice it to say, I'm fed up with the negative influences of our culture on women. The magazines, however, are only part of the problem. Add television, movies, and music, and our daughters are bombarded with smut from the moment they wake up to the moment they go to bed.

—Vicki Courtney, founder of Virtuous Reality Ministries[9]

RECENT BELIEVE IT OR NOTS

If you scout around enough, you will soon learn that when it comes to periodicals, what you think you are going to get isn't necessarily what you will get. I learned this lesson the hard way when Jessica was a mid- to older teen. I bought her a subscription to *Seventeen* as a little surprise gift. Well, I was the one who got the surprise. One afternoon, while cleaning her room (which is another story within itself), the phone rang. I answered the nearby extension, sat on her bed to chat, and began to flip nonchalantly through an issue of the magazine that had been left nearby on the floor. If I remember correctly, it was a little article about sexual pleasure that made me realize that her *Seventeen* and my *Seventeen* were two different animals!

As Jessica and I began researching for this book, I purchased a copy of *Teen Voices*, which has the tag line "Because you're more than just a pretty face." The cover featured three prepubescent girls, one still wearing braces, none of them old enough to have breasts. I was immediately curious about this magazine, especially when my eye caught the lead story: "Virginity: Why All the Hype?" Within the context of the article are lines like, "But having sex doesn't have to be ... scary if the decision is yours, if you use the right protection ... and if you fully trust the person you are interested in having sex with." In answer to the question, "What's up with guys wanting a virgin?" your young daughters can read, "Many cultures and religious beliefs state that it's very important for girls to keep their virginity until they are married. This whole deal comes from the idea that men own women."[10]

Ironically, at the back of the magazine was a story titled "Why Am I Sad?" which was tag-lined "Understanding Postpartum Depression."

However, online reviews and comments from teen girls are favorable because the magazine, they say, is not about boys, cosmetics, and clothes. *Teen Voices* hits hard issues such as rape, what to expect during a gynecological visit, sexism, racism, and issues concerning being too self-conscious.

Seventeen has clearly become an "older teen" magazine. In a recent issue, a "sex survey" was conducted by the Kaiser Family Foundation, which was then followed by the results,[11] revealing facts like the following:

- Thirty percent of virgins fifteen to seventeen years of age have "been intimate."
- Over 40 percent of guys fifteen to seventeen years of age have had two to five sexual partners.

- Just under 40 percent of girls fifteen to seventeen years of age have had two to five sexual partners.

- Thirty percent of sexually active guys and 49 percent of sexually active girls ages fifteen to seventeen have had sex without a condom.

- Thirty-three percent of sexually active girls have had oral sex in order to avoid having intercourse.

A recent issue of *Jane* magazine had a short clip about sexual spanking, saying "I love you" for the first time during orgasm, and sexual positions to aid the "little fella." (There was also an ad for skinny-dipping and another for clothing featuring a completely naked woman.)

However, one of the most disappointing magazines, on a personal level, has been *Guideposts Sweet 16*. While away on business I picked up this slick-covered magazine and began flipping through the pages. The August/September issue offered back-to-school fashion and the typical polls and quizzes and "embarrassing moments."

Though I would give *GP Sweet 16* a fairly high rating, parents still should read all of its content. For example, in an advice column, a young "advice-giving guy" suggests "dating before hooking up." The problem with this counsel is that "hooking up" could mean anything from passionate petting to actual sex, according to the teen using it. "Avoid being physical until you two are dating"[12] can sound like an okay for sex after a few weeks of going to the movies or McDonald's or something.

It isn't much better for "guy magazines" either. Recently, Jessica came to me, hands on hips and a stern look on her face. "Have you seen where they're positioning the magazines for men at convenience stores these days?"

I assured her that I had. "It's not just that they're using sex to advertise everything," she said, "but do they have to put half-naked women on the covers and then stack the magazines where children can see?"

A few weeks later, she entered our home with a few of the top magazines for guys. And she was right. Never in my life have I seen so much flesh to advertise so much that has nothing to do with flesh. What's more, we are not talking about "girly magazines," but just "plain ol' magazines" that most guys would appreciate.

Even teen and preteen guys.

How to Talk to Your Girls about Fashion/Teen Magazines

As distressing as it may seem, you will not—in all probability—be able to keep your daughters away from magazines. Even if you don't subscribe, chances are they'll pick one up in a doctor's office, at a girlfriend's house, or even at school. In the end, we all know that girls talk about fashion. They talk about makeup. They talk about boys. And they talk about sex. Therefore, magazines are going to appeal to them. So, while I encourage you to be age-appropriate conscious, use magazines as a starting point to establish dialogue that will help them make positive decisions.

But there are other issues that you should address. One thing you will note (and you'll want to point out to your daughters) is that most magazine models don't look that way in real life. Most fashion model photographs have been "doctored"—in other words, airbrushed. In fact, in some cases, inches of flesh have been removed. Legs have been sculpted. Arm flab has been reduced. Under-eye circles have been magically taken away. Acne has been erased without the aid of medical science or over-the-counter products. Hair, perfectly coiffed, was styled by a team of professionals. Makeup was applied by those who have studied the absolute art of application. And, finally, "Just because a dress looks good on her doesn't mean you have the body type for it, sweetheart, so let's look for a style that does flatter your particular figure." Positive moments!

You will also want to note that fashion magazines meant for younger and older women are loaded with ads for alcoholic beverages (typically showing a bunch of beautiful people having fun on a beach, against the allure of a New York skyline, and so forth) and also for tobacco products like cigarettes. (I have never seen an ad showing a blackened lung, a wrinkled face, or fingers yellowed from the effects of nicotine. Nor do advertisers use photographs that convey the "pleasure" of ashtray breath. But wouldn't that be interesting?) You will also notice that a lot of advertisers are selling their wares by use of nudity. Everything from watches to shaving cream to clothing (an oxymoron if there ever was one) is sold by way of nakedness; the idea seems to be that everything can be sold by the use of sexuality.

According to a teen magazine report, 35 percent of U.S. girls six to twelve years of age have been on at least one diet, and 50 to 70 percent of them, though normal in weight, consider themselves overweight.[13]

But more than these types of advertisements, you will want to be aware of the mixed messages from the ads and articles combined. In an article for Women's E-news (womensenews.org), commentator Sheila Gibbons discusses the quandary of teen girls as they read teen magazines. She writes, "The yin and yang of being simultaneously irresistible and virginal fill page after page. Impressionable teens (and pre-teens) are being whip-sawed by the mixed messages."[14]

In other words, carefully study the content of the magazines your daughters read. Make sure that there is a balance of messages sent and received. For example, your daughters need to understand the difference between a healthy diet and dangerous fad diets; and that as princesses (daughters of the King), their sexuality is meant for the bedroom of their marriage, that it is sacred and will be beautiful, but it is not for parading about and discussion on slick pages of periodicals.

How to Talk to Your Boys about "Girly" Magazines

There is a world of difference in "girl" magazines and "girly" magazines. Girl magazines tend to confuse young women about their sexuality within God's design. Girly magazines are pretty much clear on one issue: women are to be seen only as sexual beings rather than as equal partners with men the way God designed them to be.

The dangers of print porn are valid. I want to remind you of an extreme case, but one that was very real nonetheless. His name was Theodore Robert Cowell, but most of us remember him as "Ted Bundy, serial killer." Between 1974 and 1979, in just five short years, Bundy sexually assaulted and then killed between thirty and one hundred young girls and women, one as young as twelve years old.

A sick, sick man? Yes. But if you are imagining a devil with horns, think again. Ted Bundy was, at one time, a Boy Scout. He was once an assistant director of the Seattle Crime Prevention advisory committee and even wrote a pamphlet instructing women on rape prevention.[15] He was handsome, witty, highly intelligent, and loved. He was even deemed a hero for saving the life of a three-year-old boy in Washington state.

The night before he was executed on January 24, 1989, Ted Bundy gave an interview to Dr. James Dobson of Focus on the Family. In the later-televised meeting, Bundy made no excuses for his behavior, but he did, however, issue a chilling warning to parents everywhere when he spoke of the day he and some friends found pornographic magazines in a trashcan and began exploring the world of women, flesh, and sexual misconduct.

SO TELL YOUR SONS ...

"WWJD?" I know it's a cliché, but try asking your sons, "Would Jesus look at this particular magazine? If not, why are you looking at it?" Remind them that as Christians we are to "be imitators of God" (Eph. 5:1).

"Guard your heart." Solomon, in his wisdom, said, "My son, pay attention to what I say; listen closely to my words.... they are life to those who find them and health to *a man's whole body.* Above all else, guard your heart, for it is the wellspring of life" (Prov. 4:20, 22–23). How does a young man guard his heart? By guarding his eyes. In the same passage, Solomon wrote, "Let your eyes look straight ahead, fix your gaze directly before you" (v. 25). Tell them to keep their eyes on Jesus. (See Heb. 12:2.)

"Ask yourself, 'What if this were my sister? My mother? My future wife?'" Respect is more than the title of an Aretha Franklin song. As one father put it, "Respect is a real and tangible thing."

"I know, I understand, I've been there too." Father, when you speak to your sons, speak openly about understanding the nature of the temptation. You have been there too, and if you think about it, I'm sure you can remember the spiritual tug-of-war raging daily within your own body. (Allow me to interject here how

There's no question about it. The FBI's own study on serial homicide shows that the most common interest among serial killers is pornography. Well-meaning, decent people will condemn the behavior of a Ted Bundy, while they're walking past a magazine rack full of the very kinds of things that send young kids down the road to be Ted Bundys. But I'll tell you, there are lots of other kids playing in streets around this country today who are going to be dead tomorrow, and the next day, and the next day and month, because other young people are reading the kinds of things and seeing the kinds of things that are available in the media today.

—Ted Bundy[16]

vital it is that you have gained control over your own temptations and lusts. To expect anything more from your sons than you are willing to give is hypocritical at best.) Give them the opportunity for accountability with you: not judgment, but accountability. Having sexual desires is normal; remember that fact. Focusing that desire onto slick paper with airbrushed images is not normal.

"It's adultery, son." Jesus said, "But I tell you that anyone who looks at a woman lustfully has already committed adultery with her in his heart" (Matt. 5:28). Looking at magazines loaded with naked women in sultry poses isn't about love. It's about lust. And lust, according to our Lord, is adultery. Adultery, according to the Word of God, is damnable.

"Who owns whom here?" In his book *Spit and Polish for Husbands,* author Bryan Davis makes a slightly comical though hard-hitting point. "Let's get real, guys," he writes. "What's this pornography stuff all about, anyway? Freak shows aside, more than ninety-nine percent of the women in these pictures look pretty much alike ... breasts are in front, buttocks are in back, there are two arms and two legs, and an epidermis holds it all together.... And we won't conquer these women; they're untouchable. In fact, if we lust after them, they've conquered us. We've fallen into their trap."[18]

There is another kind of adulterous woman who lurks in the shadows, quiet and unseen.... yet she is more alluring than the street harlot and just as destructive as the motel tryst.... Although she wears no clothes, she bears a sword, ready to cut your heart in two, setting body in conflict with spirit. She is ... pornography.

—Bryan Davis, *Spit and Polish for Husbands*[17]

"Remember the Lord in your youth." Another wise word from Solomon: "Remember your Creator in the days of your youth, before the days of trouble come and the years approach when

you will say, 'I find no pleasure in them'" (Eccl. 12:1). Remind your sons that conquering the desire to view magazine porn (or any porn for that matter) will not get easier when they get older or when they get married. The images they are allowing to be seared into their impressionable brains will only add fuel to the flame, not quench it. (We will talk more about this subject in a later chapter.)

A Word (or Two) to Mom

Yes, Mom, you.

Word One: You may be a single mother, and your children's father may not be in the picture at all. If he is not, and you have a male role model you trust to talk with your sons, I encourage you to ask him to do so. Friends, relatives, and pastors are available to help you with this delicate issue. But don't shy away from it if you are alone in this thing we call parenting. The devil isn't afraid to come on to your sons; you shouldn't be coy about having a direct conversation (and future accountability conversations) with your boys.

Word Two: Be careful about the magazines that arrive with your name addressed on them. How many Victoria's Secret catalogs come to your mailbox? And please don't think you can get them and hide them and your sons won't know. Many a boy cut his sexual teeth on "hidden" porn magazines. How about *Redbook, Cosmo,* or other women's magazines that give "instruction" on sexuality? Keeping your sons pure from lustful images begins with you, too.

Now Showing on a Magazine Shelf Near You (A Parent's Guide)

According to AllYouCanRead.com, the following magazines are the most popular magazines for teens and tweens (whether marketed for them or not).[19] We have compiled them (in alphabetical order) with an explanation of their contents along with Web sites for parental guidance before purchasing.

AMERICAN GIRL

Created especially for girls ages seven and up, *American Girl* is an appealing, age-appropriate alternative to teen magazines. It features advice, crafts, contests, puzzles, games, giggles, and more! It includes stories, games, party plans, contests, sports tips, and more for girls seven to twelve. Its Web site also includes resources in age-appropriate categories for mothers. (www.AmericanGirl.com)

BOY CRAZY!

Boy Crazy! is the first magazine written by boys for girls. According to an online letter from the editor, it gives girls an "unprecedented access into the minds of real, everyday boys."[20] Each year one hundred boys are profiled, and questions are raised and answered so as to give girls—ages twelve to seventeen—a better understanding of the opposite sex. (www.BoyCrazy.com)

BOY'S LIFE

The official magazine of the Boy Scouts of America, *Boy's Life* covers everything from Scouting itself to sports, health, hobbies, and so forth. *Boy's Life* is targeted for boys ages seven to seventeen, though remarks at www.Amazon.com indicate that it is best for younger (Cub Scout) readers. (www.BoysLife.org)

CAMPUS LIFE

CL is published by Christianity Today and is about keeping God first in everyday teen issues, especially those issues teens deal with in high school and college. Though considered a "Christian magazine," *CL* examines tough "every man's" issues like dating, sex, and cursing. (www.CampusLife.org)

CosmoGIRL!

CosmoGIRL! is the "younger sister" of *Cosmopolitan* and covers issues more appropriate for the teen age-group. There are slick ads for high-priced fashion as well as over-the-counter products and articles about everything from celebrities to sexuality. (www.CosmoGirl.com)

COSMOPOLITAN
(RATED THE NUMBER TWELVE MAGAZINE BY ALLYOUCANREAD.COM)

Cosmo is not targeted to teens, but teenage girls rate it high among their periodical choices anyway. Parents may want to take a look at the editorial reviews at www.Amazon.com, which state, "*Cosmopolitan* (or as it's affectionately known, *Cosmo*) has sex on the brain. Hugh Hefner is a monk compared to the Cosmo Girl in the fun fantasy world conjured by the magazine. The naughty cover headlines ('151,497 of You Begged to See THIS Guy Butt Naked') are legendary, veritable haikus of horniness reportedly perfected by David Brown, the movie-producer husband of *Cosmo's* most famous editor, Helen Gurley Brown."[21] (www.Cosmopolitan.com)

DISCOVERY GIRL

DG is for the younger female readers in your home. It was created for and by girls ages seven to twelve and is a forum for girls within this age bracket to express their thoughts and ideas on issues relative to them. (www.DiscoveryGirl.com)

ELLE GIRL

Another "baby sister" magazine, *Elle Girl* is the younger version of the long-standing *Elle*. Fashion, makeup, and living life as a girl all over the world are featured. Amazon.com reviews are highly favorable, including a note from one girl expressing her joy that the magazine is not filled with articles and stories about having sex. (www.ElleGirl.com)

GIRL'S LIFE

Unlike *Boy's Life*, this magazine is not a part of Scouting. It is highly rated by readers, has won numerous Parents' Choice Awards (among others), and is for girls ages ten and up, though probably more for younger readers. *Girl's Life* has a readership of more than three million girls and covers everything from advice about fashion and boys to bedroom makeovers. It has received some online rebuke, however, for being too WASP. (www.GirlsLife.com)

GUIDEPOSTS FOR TEENS / GUIDEPOSTS SWEET 16

Guideposts magazine has entertained readers for as long as most of us can remember. In fact, some of us can remember our grandparents reading the little magazine that packs a whole lot of punch. It is important to note, however, that *Guideposts* is an inter-faith magazine and, like its "parent," so is *Guideposts for Teens*, which—after six years—became *Guideposts Sweet 16*. They are highly recommended, though I would suggest that parents not take the name at face value (see "Recent Believe It Or Nots" on page 131). (www.GuidepostsSweet16mag.com)

JANE

Jane is another "women's" magazine (for ages eighteen to thirty-four) that has popularity among today's younger teen girls as well. Articles cover everything from fashion and beauty to sex and the Internet. (www.JaneMagazine.com/2001)

MARIE CLAIRE

MC, like *Jane*, is for women, though young teens enjoy flipping through the glossy ad-filled pages, which disclose the skinny (and then some) on topics of women's concerns. Amazon.com's editorial calls it a "grab bag" of hot issues (war, sex, fashion, and so forth), and that bag has made *Marie Claire* a long-running favorite (established in 1937) as well as an international delight. (www.MarieClaire.com)

MAXIM

(RATED THE NUMBER ONE MAGAZINE BY ALLYOUCANREAD.COM)

Maxim is most definitely not for boys but is still highly read by them. Think *Playboy*, but perhaps a bit tamer. This is a men's magazine, though it can often be found at a child's eye-level in convenience stores. *Maxim* does have a Web site, which offers soft-porn and therefore will not be listed here (though your teenagers may have already found it).

NEW MOON

New Moon is for and by girls, ages eight to fourteen. Tag line: "The Magazine for Girls and Their Dreams." The magazine's Web site declares two important issues for Christian parents to note. (1) *NM* is the six-time recipient of the Parents' Choice Gold Award. (2) At the time of this writing, the tag line at the Web site read, "New Moon Magazine for Girls: smart feminist girl's magazines." (www.newmoon.org)

PLAYBOY

(RATED THE NUMBER ELEVEN MAGAZINE BY ALLYOUCANREAD.COM)

Like *Maxim*, *Playboy* is not a magazine for boys or young men but is fashioned toward the adult male. Because of *Playboy's* history, no further description or Web site listing (which also contains free soft-porn) is necessary to the purpose of this book.

SEVENTEEN

On shelves and in the hands of young girls since 1944, *Seventeen* has evolved in a lot of ways. Though called *Seventeen*, the target audience is late teens to early twenties. In spite of this fact, *Seventeen* tends to be read by younger audiences, though some of the subject matter is not appropriate, such as the sexuality polls. (www.Seventeen.com)

STUFF

(RATED THE NUMBER TEN MAGAZINE BY ALLYOUCANREAD.COM)

A lot like *Maxim* and *Playboy*, but with a little more silliness and humor thrown in, *Stuff* is for grown men, not boys or teens. For the same reasons that we held out information or detail on *Maxim* and *Playboy*, we will leave *Stuff*'s description incomplete here.

TEEN

Tag-lined "What being a TEEN is all about," *Teen* features the latest trends and info on fashion, beauty, boys, dating, celebrities, quizzes, and horoscopes. Slated for girls ages twelve to nineteen. (www.TeenMag.com)

TEEN PEOPLE

Teen People is another youth-focused magazine spawned from the adult version. Reviews at Amazon.com range from "not for anyone with religious beliefs" to "amazing ... for the in-crowd teens." *TP* apparently goes beyond just celebrity news, diving into fashion and youth culture issues as well. (www.TeenPeople.com)

You may not want to know this, but teens are having sex.

—Seen at TeenVoices.com[22]

TEEN VOGUE

The ultimate style and trend magazine goes younger. Think *Vogue*, but with the average (rich) teen in mind. If your daughters enjoy slick ads, over-the-top cosmetics, Louis Vuitton, fashion to the extreme, and actually know what D and G stands for, then *Teen Vogue* is for them. (www.TeenVogue.com)

TEEN VOICES

Teen Voices is highly praised by readers as being full of "meat" rather than just fashion gravy. I will continue to voice, however, a word of warning to mothers who get this magazine for their daughters. The covers often appear to be for tweens, but the magazine does address deep sexual issues such as masturbation, oral sex, homosexuality, and teen pregnancy. (www.TeenVoices.com)

TWIST

Twist is celebrity driven—whether those celebrities are from the movies, music, or television—and caters to teens (girls, mainly) ages twelve to seventeen. Sex is a driving issue (with articles like "The Truth about Sex Myths"), and daily horoscopes can be read. The Web site includes tarot readings as well, however, and parents will want to be aware of this fact. (www.TwistMagazine.com)

YM (YOUR MAGAZINE)

YM is the hot ticket when it comes to teen (mainly girls) magazines. Just about everything is found within its pages: fun, fashion, dating advice, fiction, and teen-interest articles. (www.YM.com)

CHAPTER 6

Just a Mouse Click Away ...

The Internet, Sex, and Your Children

"You have heard that it was said, 'Do not commit adultery.' But I tell you that anyone who looks at a woman lustfully has already committed adultery with her in his heart."

—MATTHEW 5:27–28

So here's the joke: When my husband first brought a computer into our home—back in about 1990—I pitched what we in the South call a "hissy fit."

"Why would I want that thing in our house?" I cried. I thought PCs were both ugly (didn't go with my English country style at all) and unnecessary.

Who would have known that within ten years I would be making a living (not to mention a lifestyle) off one? Thus, the joke.

I "live" on the Internet. (There, and, it has been noted, in a few jewelry departments of well-known department stores.) When I am asked about my favorite sites, I always mention places like www.Crosswalk.com, www.Biblegateway.com, and www.Bibleplaces.com. These are the places I can go to study the Word of God, to get the latest articles from the people I respect within ministry, and to look at the landscapes of my favorite place in the world, Israel.

For your children, the Internet can be a wonderful learning tool. They can receive help with their homework, read books, and even connect with family and friends who live hundreds and even thousands of miles away. They can learn about other countries and their cultures by actually "chatting" with their citizens.

But like everything else, there are issues surrounding the Internet that could be harmful to children—specifically, Internet pornography and child exploitation.

WHAT IS INTERNET PORN?

I recently heard the following analogy: parents who would never dream of dropping their children off in the middle of Times Square, with all its cultural offerings, to leave them to tour it solo, are virtually (pun intended) doing so every single day when they allow them to surf the Internet unsupervised.

Currently, there are more than 300,000 pornographic Web sites on the Internet, according to David Burt of N2H2 (a Seattle, Washington-based Web-filtering company), and this number is growing every day.[1] And it is not something your children have to go in search of on their own. It can come to them. A 2001 Kaiser Family Foundation study found that 70 percent of teens (ages fifteen to seventeen) had "accidentally come across" pornography while on the Internet.[2] According to a survey conducted by the National Academies, one in four children reported at least one unwanted exposure to sexually explicit pictures during the past year, and one out of five reported receiving a sexual solicitation.[3] In the United Kingdom a recent report warned parents that they should be on guard when it comes to their children and the Internet. In this particular case, researchers interviewed more than 1,500 children, ages nine to nineteen, and discovered that nearly 60 percent had come into contact with porn. Out of the 969 parents interviewed, only one in twenty was aware of this situation. In fact, according to the report, only 16 percent of the parents were even aware that their children had ever seen online porn.[4] And, unbeknownst to most parents, more than half of the children interviewed said they had given out personal information while online.[5]

Pornography, according to *Merriam-Webster's Online Dictionary,* is defined as

1. the depiction of erotic behavior (as in pictures or writing) intended to cause sexual excitement; material (as books or a photograph) that depicts erotic behavior and is intended to cause sexual excitement
2. the depiction of acts in a sensational manner so as to arouse a quick intense emotional reaction.

The gap between what children are actually doing and what their parents think they are doing is a lot larger than many people would have imagined. It is a gap we must try to close.

—John Carr, Internet Adviser[6]

Internet porn is, by obvious definition, pornography that is viewed or sold across the "Superhighway" of "the Web," which I find to be an appropriate title here. If you spend any time at all researching I-Porn (as it is often called), you will come to a fast conclusion: it is here to stay—it's not going anywhere—and the government seems powerless against it.

Parent, when it comes to protecting your children from Internet pornography, it's really up to you.

JUST A MOUSE CLICK AWAY

With just one mouse click your children's view of sex can be altered forever.

The stories are too numerous to count: children online who "accidentally" come upon a porn site. Truly, they don't mean to do it. But take note: the porn kings know exactly what they are doing and who will be affected when they set up their sites.

One of the most infamous sites for tripping children has to

do with the one of the most famous government buildings in America. As students work on school projects and reports, they will—in this day and time—go to the Internet for research and support. By typing in the name of this institution (which will go unnamed, but believe me will be on their lists of places to learn about as they study American history), they will be taken to a Web site considered to be the "#1 adult entertainment site on the Web." With the click of a mouse, they will be taken to a page adorned with half-naked girls, still shots of couples having inter-course, and insinuations of lesbian sex. The "free preview" leaves nothing to the imagination, densely populated with hyperlinks that read, "Barely 18 Girl/Girl Live," "Teen Sex Channel Movies," and "Teen Buffet." There is even a "free for all" area where children can see still shots of couples in their most private moments, couples—both same sex and male/female—who have allowed Web cams to be placed in their homes for the viewers' pleasure. And those viewers can easily be your children.

There are other methods for luring children into the porno-graphic web, methods that have become illegal under a provi-sion of the Amber Alert legislation that makes it a crime to use misleading Web addresses to draw children to porn. What these sites are known for is switching a couple of letters in a Web site address, using phrases common to children such as the names of icons, games, dolls and other toys, and even sports.

The fact of the matter is that there was a time not so long ago when parents warned their children about walking up to strange cars and instructed them to run from men who beseeched them to "help me find my puppy," or who asked, "Would you like a piece of candy?" Today's parents have a new predator to worry about, and it is not found on street corners and in dark alleys. This one resides in their homes, sits innocently waiting at public libraries, and rests atop desks in both public and private schools.

There is something else parents may want to know about. It is called "mousetrapping." Simply put, mouse-trapping is a method used by porn software engineers to keep viewers within their pornographic snares. Once visitors to one of the Web sites are in, they find that they can't get out.

It works like this. Suppose one of your children innocently types a Web site address into a search engine. The page shifts and *voilà!* porn. As previously instructed by you, your son or daughter attempts to click the X in order to get out of the site, but instead ends up in another porn site, which is, in reality, a part of the first. Another click of the X, and another site comes up, this one more revealing than the last. And so on, and so on.

According to "NetValue Report on Minors Online" (*Business Wire,* 12/19/00), three million of the unique visitors to adult Web sites in September 2000 were age seventeen or younger. Slightly more than 21 percent of the minors who visited these sites were fourteen or younger.

—Internet Safety Brochure, National Coalition for the Protection of Children and Families

Mousetrapping. The bait is out, the trap is set, and guess who is the mouse? Your child.

So what should you tell your children to do if they find themselves in such a predicament? Easy enough: come and find you. In the case of mousetrapping, your computer will most likely need to be shut down and then restarted, something you probably wouldn't want younger children to attempt.

Of course Internet porn isn't found only by tripping fingers leading to saucy Web sites; it can also come in the form of an email or IM (instant message), headed up by graphic subject lines. Invitations that read, "Hi, I'm Meghan, and I recently talked with a friend of yours who said you're really cool. If you wanna see me and my best friend in our new dorm room, click

I am confident that every child is contacted by a sexual predator at one point or another. If they talk online, especially in chat rooms, they will be contacted by at least one, 100 percent of the time. It doesn't matter where your computer is set up or how much you monitor what they do while online.

—Keith Dunn[7]

here." Invitations like this one are oftentimes more than an adult male can handle, much less a teenage boy with raging hormones. And for the innocent eight-year-old ... well, it's just too easy.

If you think the spammers care who receive their enticing lines, think again. Spammers, those who send these unsolicited mass emailings, have no concerns about the age or sensitivities of the recipients. To them, it is just another day at the office.

THE DANGER OF CHAT ROOMS AND INSTANT MESSAGES

Chat rooms can be fun. In fact, if it weren't for a chat room, I might not be sitting here right now writing this book. Back in the early part of 1999, someone told me about a group known as CLASS (Christian Leaders, Authors, Speakers Services)[8] and a weekly chat room where one could go and chat with other Christians who were either authors and speakers or prayed to be. I was one who prayed to be, so I went. There I met women and men who are, today, among my dearest friends, and a few in particular who helped give birth to my ministry.

Chat rooms can be fun. But they can be dangerous as well.

Children, especially those who may be shy or have social anxieties, are eager to find acceptance in chat rooms and through instant messages. First, allow me to define "chat room" and "instant message" in case you don't know what these terms mean. According to www.GetNetWise.org, "chat room" is the name given to a place or page in a Web site or online service where people can "chat" with each other by typing messages that are displayed almost instantly on the screens of others who are in the same "chat room"; an "instant message," or IM, is technology similar to that of chat rooms, which notifies users when a friend is online, allowing them to "converse" by exchanging text messages.[9] These text messages come in the form of little boxes, sometimes complete with "wallpaper," "icons," "sound," "smileys" and "away messages." The most-used IM service worldwide is AOL (America Online) and AOL's AIM (AOL Instant Messaging). In 2003, America Online predicted that by 2005 IMs would surpass email as the primary way of communicating online.[10]

According to NetValue, children spent nearly 70 percent more time on porn sites than game sites.

—The NetValue Report on Minors Online[11]

One thing most parents know for sure, a child who can't carry on anything above a monosyllabic conversation can manage multiple IMs (one mother reported her child boasts of being able to handle up to twenty at a time) while, at the same time, chatting in a chat room. I have spoken to parents who chuckle as they tell me they often walk up behind their child to "check on who they're talking to online," only to discover it's their child's friend who lives next door or down the street.

Sometimes, however, it is not a friend the child is talking to; it is a potential threat to the child's safety. The most common and easiest way for a sexual predator to reach your children is through chat rooms and IMs. One characteristic in children that online predators look for little parental involvement. This man (or, in some cases, woman) may come across as a same-age peer or as an adult who "understands their needs."

While chat rooms are public and can be witnessed by many, IMs are private, typically witnessed only by the two parties involved in the exchange. When one of your children is in a chat room, he or she can be IM'd by one of the chat room participants asking if the child wants to go into a "private room." This enables the two to get to know each other better, chatting one-on-one rather than above the "cacophony" of the chat room. And believe me, it can get pretty "loud" in there.

If your child is the "invitee," and the "inviter" is of the same age-group, wanting to share personal info such as favorite songs, movies, books, and so forth, then chances are your child is safe. It is pretty much the same as if he or she had gone to a party, met a new friend in a room full of peers, slipped over to a quiet corner of the room, and began chatting. But if this person is not really a peer, your child is in danger. Unlike the personal chat at the party, there is no way to truly know unless the child sees the person eyeball to eyeball.

Parent, one thing you should always be aware of: There are people out there who are willing to invest a large amount of time, effort, and energy into getting your children to talk to them, trust them, confide in them, and then have sex with them—virtual or otherwise. They are not above sending gifts, being so brazen as to send them to your home, right under your nose. The stories of children being suddenly swept into the imaginary world of cybersex (sexual arousal involving communication on the Internet) are too real and too many. There is, for example, the case of Daniel Fecteau. While chatting online, Fecteau convinced fifteen-year-old Heather Scott that he was a seventeen-year-old boy. He was, in fact, nearly fifty. Telling her he had purchased jewelry and a car for her, he managed to convince Heather to fly from her home in Modesto, California, back to Maine with him. Fortunately, when Heather's mother became suspicious of her absence, authorities were called, and the couple was stopped at the Sacramento International Airport.

Even more upsetting is the case of Daniel Alonzo Smith, who sexually abused a fifteen-year-old girl, then forced her to go online in order to lure other children for him. Using a Web cam (Web camera), the victim initiated sexual dialogue by showing her breasts, inviting a thirteen-year-old girl to have sex with her, and then asking if she would be interested in a relation-

[It is reported that] 89 percent of sexual solicitations were made in either chat rooms or Instant Messages.

—Pew Study reported in JAMA, 2001[12]

ship with an older man (which would, of course, be Smith). Smith, who aided the first victim with her typing, was surely stunned when he learned the thirteen-year-old would-be victim was actually an agent with the Utah Internet Crimes Against Children Task Force.

But what if "she" hadn't been?

THE TRUTH ABOUT CHRISTIAN CHAT ROOMS

Yes, parent, there are Christian chat rooms and even Christian chat rooms for teens, a place where your youth can talk about their prayer needs—school, relationships, parents, and so forth, on a spiritual level. And, just as in adult Christian chat rooms, non-Christians can infiltrate them—people who want to sow seeds of confusion or dissention.

BLOGGING

"Blogging" is a fairly new word. In fact, my spell-checker insists that it is not even a word. But for those who are tech-savvy—like your children for instance—it is. A blog is an Internet diary; blogging is the actual writing of the blog. Blogs are places where kids and teens can share their innermost feelings or show off their writing skills, poetry, and so forth. And, once again, they are places where children can find themselves in a world of sexual stimuli.

Not all blogs are sexual; in fact, those who understand blogging best say sexual blogging is not yet that common. Given time, however, we may have another story to tell. The most common blogging site for teens (they have to be at least thirteen years of age to join) is www.Xanga.com, which has free membership and open posting. Here, teens can talk about school, relationships, parents, the movies they are watching, or the music they are listening to.

That said, it is important to remind your children that if they are blogging personal thoughts on the Internet, those thoughts can be seen and read by anyone at any time. Other teens may read and respond, but the blog is a perfect viewing perch for the predator as well. The more your children say about themselves, the more information the predator has to begin dialoguing with them.

ADULTS AND THEIR DIRTY LITTLE SECRETS
(WHY SOME TEENS WON'T LISTEN)

My friend Jack Samad (with the National Coalition for the Protection of Children and Families) shocked me with the story of his attendance at a religious convention. The manager of the hotel where he had been staying noticed the posters and other paraphernalia he had carried through the lobby early one morning and then back in again later that afternoon. He stopped Jack and asked him what he was doing with all that information on pornography. Jack told him he was a part of the Christian conference being held in that city. The manager chuckled. "Get real," he said. "Porn movies in our hotel are accessed at a higher rate during Christian conventions than at any other time."

It's true. In a recent article for *Today's Christian Woman* titled "Dirty Little Secret," writer Ramona Richards disclosed a shocker within the very first line. Thirty-four percent of the female *TCW* online newsletter readers admitted to intentionally accessing Internet porn. Apparently online sex addiction isn't just a male problem anymore; these women are wives, moms, and sisters who all profess faith in Jesus Christ.[13]

I don't use the word *addiction* lightly. Scientists have proved that the use of porn causes the brain to release endorphins, giving the viewer much the same euphoric experience as a drug addict using crack cocaine. And, like crack, it creates the need for "higher hits" in order to satisfy. This is why Internet porn sites are able to give viewers a free show, knowing that once they are in, they will want—no, need—more. They, or their children, will find some way to fork over the $1.00, $2.95, or $4.95 in order to go a little bit deeper into a web that is difficult to break free of once they are caught up in it. Happily for the porn kings—but cautionary for parents—is the fact that Internet porn is available all day, all night, all the time.

Another pastor fell this week to infidelity, and it began with porn on the Internet. There are men who wouldn't think about mainlining heroin, who wouldn't think about picking up a needle and shooting heroin into [their] arm, who wouldn't think about smoking crack cocaine, but [who] will view porn on the Internet and think to [themselves], "This isn't addictive" when it is every bit as addictive as heroin or crack cocaine. Why? Because there's a little voice inside saying, "What? Is it gonna kill ya?"

—Dr. Joel Hunter[14]

Since it is so easy to become ensnared, is it any wonder that more than 50 percent of evangelical pastors report they viewed pornography last year? Or that 50 percent of Promise Keepers attendees viewed porn within a week before the event?[15]

If the men and women—the adults our children look up to—who sit in our church pews or stand behind the pulpits on

Sundays are struggling with Internet pornography, how can we expect our youth to resist it? Do we truly trust their young judgment when it comes to such intensely important matters? Or do we, as their parents, choose to maintain a constant watch over their precious, impressionable lives, knowing that what they see in a matter of seconds will be forever burned into their brains?

Whether drawn in by curiosity or caught off guard by images that pop up unexpectedly, thousands of people of all ages, backgrounds, and religious beliefs are becoming victims of the deadly disease of pornography.

—Sean Dunn,
Momentum: Gaining Ground with God [16]

THE TRUTH BEHIND FIREWALLS, FILTERS, BLOCKS, AND COMPUTER LOCATIONS

Many parents have elected to install firewalls, blocks, and other filtering technology in their computers in order to thwart solicitation and/or the accidental or nonaccidental viewing of pornography by their children while surfing the Internet. Web sites such as the one for the National Coalition for the Protection of Children and Families (http://nationalcoalition.org/) offer a filter review site (www.FilterReview.com) that helps parents determine the system best for their individual and family needs. Sites such as www.ProtectKids.com, www.AFO.Net, and www.SurfControl.com (which are only three among many) offer information about specific filtering systems as well as statistics and other information about Internet safety helpful to parents.

However, it is vital to note that no filtering system is one hundred percent safe. As Jack Samad says, "A filtering system is only as effective as your child wants it to be." Meaning? "Meaning most students today know how to override the system. All it takes is a little clever maneuvering within the Internet, and they've managed to access porn."

This is so very true. In the recent interview of a high school student, I learned that while software filters are installed in her school's computers, students have quickly learned how to override them. "Porn is always being pulled up," she told me.

"And the teacher does what?" I asked.

"Looks the other way," she replied.

MOBILE MADNESS

Here's a riddle for you. What is easy to access and fits easily in a kid's pocket? Or backpack? Or purse?

Answer: cell-porn.

That's right. As if the promoters of the porn industry don't have enough to keep them busy, they can now send porn via wireless phones (and Palm Pilots) at 1.5 to 7 frames per second.

Sure, that's slow. And cell phone screens are small (about 2.5 square inches). But to a child with raging hormones and questionable wisdom, how little is too little, and how much is too much?

Currently there are more than fifty companies offering mobile porn in Europe, and analysts predict that between 2006 and 2008 this new facet to an old industry could be bringing in anywhere from $1.2 to $4 billion worldwide per year.

But can your children access it, even if they are minors? Of course they can. Though cell-porn producers say those who want to download images must be eighteen years or older, they readily admit that procedures for keeping children's hands out of the cookie jar are less than adequate. There are also news stories of children who, while attempting to download games into cell phones, have accidentally accessed Web sites for live sex, teen sex, and various other porn images.

Beyond the Web and the capabilities of downloading images from the Web is the ability of children to send images to other children (with the possibility of adults sending to children a given).

So what can you as a parent do? You can begin by making a reality check. Younger children don't need cell phones. Granted, as they get older, get jobs, or are in their cars (especially in larger cities), you may opt to purchase one for them. But ten-year-olds sporting the latest models with all their capabilities?

I don't think so.

MEET KEITH DUNN

There are hundreds of organizations designed to help keep your children safer while enjoying the benefits of the Internet. There was one in particular that fascinated me enough to pick up the telephone and call the number listed under "contact info."

Meet Keith Dunn. While in the air force, Keith served as a DARE (Drug Awareness Resistance Education) officer. Once again a civilian, he went to work as a police officer and was later hired by the Cumberland County (New Jersey) Prosecutor's Office, assigned to the Major Crimes Unit (Homicide, Sexual Assault, Indictable Juvenile Crimes). During his time there, Keith saw a TV show featuring police in Texas setting up meetings with men who wanted to have sex with kids they had met on the Internet.

"I thought, 'No way. It couldn't work in New Jersey,'" Keith tells me. "So I created a profile of a twelve-year-old girl on AOL and just left the screen name online as I went about finishing a case up. Within five minutes, I received an instant message from a twenty-two-year-old guy. He immediately wanted to meet and have sex in his car. He told me where he worked, what type of car he drove, his license plate number, and his address. He was even kind enough to give me his home and work phone numbers."

And what happened? "We met later that day at a public park where we arrested him."

From there, Keith became certified as a unit commander and member of the National Internet Crimes Against Children Task Force. He was elected as chairman of the Cumberland County Commission on Abused and Missing Children and was also a certified computer forensic examiner. He worked closely with the FBI, U.S. Customs and the U.S. Postal Service, and the National Center for Missing and Exploited Children. Today, Keith is the chairman and CEO of www.KDCOP.com, traveling across the country and speaking to school groups and other organizations, with the purpose of educating the general public on Internet safety. He has been a guest on several television shows and has served as an expert witness at trials against sexual predators.

All this by the age of twenty-eight. Yes, twenty-eight.

In speaking with Keith, the amazing thing for me was hearing how he is able to pull kids up on stage with him during a presentation and, within a matter of minutes, get their entire profile: where they go to school, what classes they take, their extracurricular activities, their home life information, and so forth.

Children are quick to give out such information, which is what sexual predators—online or otherwise—are counting on. No matter how many times we warn our children, they are simply the easiest of prey.

HOW TO TALK TO YOUR KIDS ABOUT INTERNET SAFETY

When I was a little girl, the big to-do for my brother and me was going to Kmart in Savannah with our mother. For me, a girl raised in a small town sporting little more than a "five and dime," the vast open space filled with merchandise (read: toys, records—which were about $1.99 each back then—and books) was enough to make me giddy. While my mother shopped for boring things like toilet paper and Toni Home Perms, I scanned the aisles made just for me. (This was, of course, back in the days when parents could do things like leaving their children alone in the toy department while the parents shopped around.)

More than once, I got lost. I would make my way up one aisle and then down another, slowly at first (after all, there might be something to see that I hadn't noticed yet), then a little more anxiously as I grew concerned that I had been accidentally left behind (it did happen once, but we won't get into that now). Mother and I soon came up with a plan: if we were separated for too long, we were to meet in a certain place, typically the Mattel Barbie section of the toy department.

When my daughter Jessica was little, I didn't dare let her out of my sight while shopping. This was the post–Adam Walsh era, and my fear of losing her was elevated. (Adam was the abducted and murdered six-year-old son of Reve and John Walsh. The boy's tragic death shocked the nation and led to John becoming a champion in the cause of exploited children.) But I remember telling my daughter on more than one occasion that if we were for any reason separated, she was to stand still. "As long as one of us is moving and one of us is not, I can find you. Otherwise, we might both end up going around and around in circles."

Parent, when it comes to the vast "Information Superhighway," that "big Kmart in cyberspace," you must have a plan before just "dropping your children off" there. As previously stated, I believe that one of the biggest mistakes moms and dads can make is placing a computer in a child's room or in an isolated part of the house. The risks are too high, and children are too vulnerable. So step one is to get your family computer to a safe place, if it isn't there already.

A friend of mine keeps his computer in the front of the house, his children ask permission to go online, and each night he scans the addresses of the Web sites they have visited. "It's not that I don't trust you," he tells them. "I don't trust them."

Another parent tells me that while the family computer is located in a back room of the house, her children don't know the passwords to their email addresses. "When they want to go online, their father and I are the ones to do it. And they know we are going to constantly monitor them."

Still another parent says that, even though they have Internet filters, he and his wife take no chances. "The computer is in the kitchen, which is the most commonly used room in the house. If our kids are working on a school project and need quiet, it can be arranged. But we have the passwords, so we hold the key. And we still check their activities when they're done."

In ways that have only begun to be measured, [pornography] is coloring relationships, both long- and short-term, reshaping expectations about sex and body image and, most worrisome of all, threatening to alter how young people learn about sex.

—Pamela Paul, "The Porn Factor"[17]

However you may choose to protect your children, just do it. Protect them, please. Don't believe for one second that just because you have installed software, the Internet is completely safe or that your children would never venture into places they are told not to go. (You will note in the "Christian Teens at the Round Table" section in the back of this book that teens expressed a real bafflement at their parents' trusting them as much as they do.)

Here are some other basic tips to discuss with your children and to put into practice.

If your children meet a "new friend" on the Internet—in a chat room or via an email or otherwise—and the new friend begins to ask personal questions such as "Where do you go to school?" or "What part of the country do you live in?" these are red flags. Sure, kids can ask other kids these questions, so how do you know for sure whether your children are dealing with another kid or with a predator? You don't. This is why you, as a parent, must be kept informed of every new person your children meet online. This new relationship could be a simple correspondence between "pen pals"—or it could be the start of some serious danger for your children.

In a seven to two decision handed down in May 2002, the United States Supreme Court struck down a federal law that made it a crime to create, distribute, or process "virtual" child pornography that used computer images rather than actual children, finding that the production of such material creates no real victims. In the same month, a federal appeals court in Philadelphia struck down the Children's Internet Protection Act of 2001, which required public libraries to install filtering technology to prevent access to Internet material that could be harmful to minors.

Your children should never give out personal information such as names, addresses, telephone numbers, and so forth without your knowing about it. There is absolutely nothing wrong with your children being known solely by their screen name and screen address.

Speaking of screen names, help your children determine their screen name *sans* any type of sexual innuendo. Just as you would not want your children to flirt with danger in "real space," you should not allow them to flirt with danger in cyberspace. If your children have an online profile, it should be monitored by you on a regular basis, and you should insert a note into it that reads something like this: NOTE: MY MOM AND DAD MONITOR MY ONLINE ACTIVITY. Think they will be embarrassed? Perhaps, but believe me, they would rather know that you care enough to do something to protect them than to know that you don't care enough to bother.

This kind of involvement will, of course, demand that you spend time with your children online. If you are intimidated by this new technology, use it to create a bonding time. Your kids probably know more about the computer than you do, and their sharing that knowledge with you can be fun for both of you. Also, learning more about your children's favorite online places will tell you even more about the people they are becoming.

Family details such as arguments with parents, siblings, and so forth should never be discussed. The predator will lend a listening ear, understand the situation, and then take advantage of it by moving in "for the kill." If any of your children are experiencing difficulties at home and need someone to talk to, it should be a same-sex counselor, pastor, teacher, and so forth. In addition, predators are less likely to prey upon a child who is known to be closely supervised. A child should never discuss the times when their parents may or may not be present.

If your children are younger, there should be no Internet time without your being present.

When you leave your children with a baby-sitter, the computer is not to be turned on for any reason.

If someone sends a message that concerns your children, make it clear that they are to come and get you immediately! Allow me to interject here that this is more likely to happen if your children know from an early age that they can trust you to always be there for them, to do the right thing, and to have their best interest at heart. Communication about Internet safety should begin long before words like *computer* and *Internet* are ever spoken.

Photographs should never be downloaded or uploaded without your knowledge.

Don't forget in the monitoring of your children's online activity (history files) to also check diskettes, CDs, and so forth.

Know your ISP's (Internet Service Provider's)[18] "parental controls" and "spam/porn report" provisions.

Be careful about your children's photo being posted on the Internet for sporting events, school ads, and so forth. Just as "real time" predators go to playgrounds, Internet predators go where the children are. If your children's photo is up on a Web site with pertinent information (name of school, year of graduation, hobbies, and so forth), the person on the other side of the screen has enough information to start building a relationship.

Finally, determine your personalized list of rules. Have a family meeting in which they are written out, typed up, and then posted near the computer. Include numbers for reporting the online solicitation of children or, even worse, the abduction of any of your children.

Internet safety extends beyond the borders of your home. Know the safeguards used by your children's school, the library, and the homes of your children's friends.

I would like to insert a final note here. Not everyone on the Internet is bad or wicked or evil or out to harm your children. Some "kids" really are kids, and some "kids" are not. You have to use your good judgment and discernment after having put all of the above tips into practice. A personal example involves the times when Jessica, as a young child and teenager, met several online friends who truly turned out to be nice people and who became "real time" friends. But she kept us informed of everything being said, questions being asked, and so forth. Ironically, one of her new friends lived not three blocks from our home, the two friends knew some of the same people, and they were both very active in church. When Jessica wanted to meet her new friend face-to-face, I agreed, but only after I had called a friend who already knew the person in question and I was assured that the meeting would take place with me present.

WHAT TO LOOK FOR IN YOUR CHILDREN: SIGNS OF YOUTH AND INTERNET PORN

It happens, even to the best of kids from the most Christian of homes. Kids get caught up in porn. It happened in my day with hidden *Playboy* magazines, and it happens today with the Internet. But how are you to know that one of your children has slipped into a forbidden world, blacker than black, more evil than evil? Here are a few signs there may be a problem.

- If your child spends a lot of time in chat rooms. Remember, the summer months and school vacations (such as Christmas, spring break, and so forth) are times of higher risk.

- If you find porn on your computer. Online sexual predators use photos—especially those with sexual images of adults and children to show kids that sex is normal behavior and to heighten their sexual curiosity. When checking for porn on your computer, don't forget to check CDs and diskettes.

- If your child begins receiving phone calls from adults—especially men—whom you don't know. This is another good reason not to give your young children cell phones and private lines.

- If your phone records show that your child is making calls, especially long-distance calls, to numbers you don't recognize. Remember, if your child has at least been savvy or obedient enough not to give out your phone number, there's nothing stopping the predator from giving out his: "You can't give out your phone number? I understand. That's safety. Good for you. How about if I give you mine? That way, we can talk, and you won't get in trouble."

- If your child begins receiving anonymous gifts through the mail. A predator will spend any amount of money to get to his prey. Many have sent jewelry, CDs, DVDs, and even plane tickets.

- If, when you enter the room, your child turns off the computer monitor or x's out the page being visited. Also, if you see your child communicating in chat rooms or via IMs in a "hidden language" (POS = Parents Over Shoulder; :ox = Shhh; PA= Parent Alert). When this happens, quickly ask what it means. Better yet, learn the language.

- If your child becomes withdrawn, preferring the cyber world to the real world. Such behavior may be an indication that your child has a problem with Internet porn.

CHAPTER 7

Good News for Modern Man

Hope and Help for Parents

"Only be careful, and watch yourselves closely so that you do not forget the things your eyes have seen or let them slip from your heart as long as you live. Teach them to your children and to their children after them."

—DEUTERONOMY 4:9

Don't get me wrong in all this. This really isn't a war between parents and the media, but a war that is raging "in the heavenlies." I believe with all my heart, and am convicted to state this to the bitter end, that Satan is alive and well, lives on planet Earth, and is smart enough to know that the next generation is both the most vulnerable and the most powerful.

On September 21, 1858, Abraham Lincoln stated, "The philosophy of the classroom in one generation will be the philosophy of the government in the next."[1]

Think about that statement for a moment. Ask any teacher in today's schools, and you will probably be told that education now has less to do with imparting knowledge than with trying to maintain discipline. In fact, as Jessica and I wrote this book, I randomly chatted with teachers, principals, and school officials across the country. When I told them about this project and asked them about the state of the modern classroom, their eyes rolled, and sighs escaped from deep inside their lungs. "We don't have education," one said to me. "What we have is a mess." You may recall from chapter 2, the time when one seventeen-year-old young lady named Jessica chatted with me at a Christian writers' conference. With tears in her eyes she told me of her primarily

Christian community and the school she attends. "We have computer science class, and the computers have filters, but the kids have figured out how to get around them anyway. During class they're looking at porn pictures."

"What about the teachers?" I asked her.

She shook her head. "The teachers look the other way."

In 1999, 19,000 teen sexual assaults occurred in and around school property.[2] Nineteen thousand. School hallways are patrolled by police officers. Some schools have installed metal detectors at the doorways. Children are murdering children.

At times it seems that, for the next generation, life has gone amuck even within the hallowed church buildings where young people gather together. Drive by the outside of any church on "youth night," and you will likely see students who look pretty much like any others. Many of them are tattooed, sexual fashion statements. Sometimes, if you have the opportunity to overhear their conversations, you will find that even their language doesn't set them apart from non-Christian youth.

I was recently asked to speak on the art of writing at a college near Chicago; and of course, I accepted. It was a Christian college, a place where believing young men and women are able to focus on studies in a "less secular" setting.

Nearly everything about the grounds spoke of the faith observed there, right down to the flags of Scripture that graced

When Ms. Carter walked into my office I was not prepared for the information she gave me. "My daughter ... has been sexually molested at this school." My heart jumped ... I was not prepared at all for her disturbing news. "By an adult or another student?" [I asked.] "It was another student." ... I realized we were talking about a child in our four-year-old pre-kindergarten class.

—G.W. (Bill) Reynolds III, *Sin City*[3]

the Victorian lampposts lining the sidewalks and asphalt drives snaking between imposing brick buildings and gently rolling hills.

You're getting the picture.

I was "kept" in one of the dorms. As soon as I registered and attempted to head up to my room—number 615 to be exact—I discovered that to keep the male students from fraternizing with their female counterparts, one had to use one's floor key just to push the proper floor button. This was a system, by the way, that I quickly figured a way to override.

The students attending the conference were—above all else—polite. During praise and worship their faces shone with God's glory. Oftentimes, I spotted a few of them seated on one of the wrought-iron benches, shoulders slumped and heads bent over an open Bible.

But, as I sat in the cafeteria one afternoon, I took note: the students dressed no differently than any other teens or young adults. The styles many of them chose sent a less-than-godly message.

"What makes these students," I wondered, "these Christian young adults, stand out in any crowd as believers?"

Not a thing, really … except whatever God is doing in their hearts. And when it comes to your children, that, Dad or Mom, begins with you.

ARE YOU RAISING SPIRITUAL FRUIT OR ROTTEN BANANAS?

It had been a difficult few years. Watching our daughter—our baby, the one who was our heart walking outside our bodies— as she plummeted headfirst into the world and all its trappings left us feeling helpless and alone. It seemed that every dynamic of our relationship changed, even the way she said my name.

"Mother."

What at one time had sounded like the sweetest title of honor now sounded like a curse word. To my ears, everything (or nearly everything) she said was spit out rather than spoken. Her eyes narrowed as she looked at me with contempt.

Every rule we—her father and I—attempted to force her to keep was broken. Curfews were scoffed at, leaving us to spend panic-filled nights pacing the floor, looking out the window, praying for the relief of oncoming headlights, dialing a cell phone number whose owner never answered.

Everything changed. The music she listened to, the shows she watched, the whole package. Don't get me wrong; I don't blame the media for all these changes in our daughter, but I don't blame her father or myself either. Not anymore. At first we did blame ourselves, but later—when our baby girl "returned" to us—she said something that rocked me to the very core of my being.

One evening during a heartfelt conversation, I said to her, "Daddy and I just felt as though we'd lost control."

"You couldn't lose control," she replied.

"I beg to differ," I responded quickly. "I'd tell you to be home at midnight, and you'd saunter in at five in the morning. No matter what I said, you did the opposite."

Again she said, "You couldn't lose control."

I shook my head. "Would you care to explain that?" I asked, my curiosity at its height.

And then she said the words I will never forget. "Mother," she began, the title once again a sweet endearment, "you and Daddy raised me in the Word. You couldn't lose control. That's God's promise."

Touché.

So let's get down to business. It is difficult to parent children in the age of modern media, but here are some basic suggestions that can help you.

RAISING GODLY CHILDREN

Begin by establishing God's truths as early in their little lives as possible. When Jessica was "in my tummy," I sang "Jesus Loves Me" to her every day, nearly all day long. It amazed me that, once she was born, when she cried, it took only a few measures of the song to soothe her. When I read to her, along with Mother Goose and Little Golden Books, I read biblical stories retold for children. Going to Sunday school and church was a part of her normal routine. Praying at bedtime, on the way to school, and before or during important events in her life was also normal. I wanted her to see that in every situation—no matter how small or how big—God was interested in her as a person and as his child.

As you establish God's truth in their lives, establish their relationship with him as well. "Christian" is not a title people use because they are born into a certain family or attend a particular church. Being a Christian is about living in relationship with Christ and about following his lead. Christianity is not a religion; it's a relationship. If your children are to be successful at thwarting the plans of the Enemy, they must be firmly grounded in the Lord. It is not just about who they are in him, but who he is in them. It is personal, between them and God, just as your relationship with Christ is between you and God. Your children can't get to heaven by riding on your coattails. Nor can they have an earthly relationship with Jesus by merely sidling up to you. Their relationship with God will depend on their prayer lives, their time alone with his Word, and their choices in companions and activities. Let's take each of these important ingredients one by one.

GIVING YOUR CHILDREN THEIR LIFE OF PRAYER

When you lay your infants in the crib at night, whisper prayers over them. As they grow older, teach them to make prayer a natural part of their day—and not just the first thing in the morning or the last thing before bedtime—but a natural part of their day. Show them the excitement of entering the throne room and kneeling before God, their heavenly Father. Teach them the components of prayer as Jesus taught his disciples to pray. Remind them of why they can pray to the Father, which is because of the Son. Teach them to offer up prayers of thanksgiving for all the good things in their lives as well as the difficulties. Above everything else, show them by your own example. You can't make prayer a part of their day unless it is a part of yours.

GIVING YOUR CHILDREN YOUR LIFE OF PRAYER

There are not enough words in the world to express the importance of prayer. In fact, I give prayer all the credit when it comes to opening the doors that allowed God to usher Jessica back to us, both the prayers I cried out in private and those I prayed over her personally. Allow me, if you will, to share the events I consider to be the bend in the road leading to Jessica's homecoming.

I blindly stumbled into the master bedroom, past a blue wingback chair, the dresser, and the bed, and into the seclusion of the bath. Numb, I reached into the shower and turned on the water, twisting the knob so far to the right the water would be sure to scald me. I stepped out of my clothes, pushed back the curtain, and stepped in.

For a moment, water pelted against my back, and I dropped to my knees, covering my face with my hands as a wail escaped from my very heart and soul. It was primal, really—a mother's agonizing tears of desperation. "Dear God," I finally choked out the words. "Please do whatever it takes to bring her back to your heart, but please, please don't let her die."

This was an all-too-familiar scene in those days. At some point, in the midst of it all, I buried my pride and called a girlfriend, a prayer warrior in the army of God. "I'm not even sure I know how to pray," I told her. "Even to my own ears it sounds more like begging than praying."

"Pray like this," she instructed. "Bind her will to God's will, her hands to his hands, her eyes to his eyes, her heart to his heart. Ask him to plant her feet firmly on the path he has designed for her life. And when you have done this, use the authority Jesus has given you, and loose the Enemy from doing any more harm in her life. Remind him of who you are, who she is, and who he is, which is nothing. He is a liar and a thief—he comes only to steal, kill, and destroy. But—you tell him—Jesus has come that Jessica might have life to the full!"

I scribbled my friend's words furiously and as fast as possible on a piece of scratch paper, then transferred the paper to my Bible. Every day, several times a day, I prayed this prayer, each time becoming more aware that I should have been praying this way all along, from day one, rather than waiting for a crisis.

It is not that I hadn't prayed—oh, I had! Jessica and I had prayed together at bedtime, before tests, before sports competitions. But as a part of spiritual warfare? No. I hadn't even really done spiritual warfare. So allow me to borrow from the first chapter of this book and repeat these words: parent, run to the battle line in prayer every single day in the fight for your children. And when you pray, pray specifically. Pray about those who will be of influence in their lives: friends, relatives, teachers, pastors, youth leaders, entertainment sources and icons. Pray for their strength in times of testing. And always, always pray that God will use them to influence others and to fulfill his purposes.

GIVING YOUR CHILDREN THE GIFT OF GOD'S WORD

I am in the book-writing business. And, as it were, in the book-reading business. My whole life I have loved to read, and, as my husband says, I have passed that love down to Jessica.

Jessica says that she would rather read a book than watch TV, praise God.

I am now attempting to pass that love down to my grandchildren. The kids can pretty much count on at least one book in each gift package. One of our grandchildren lives close by and, therefore, spends the night often. Every night, we read books—books about Jesus.

One day, having read everything there was to read, she brought me the *Precious Moments Bible* her "other grandma" had given her: a King James Version, no less. "Read to me, Miss Eya," she said, using her special endearment for me. My brows shot up, but she continued. "Read to me about God."

Well, I tried. I promise you I did. But we only got so far. The King James Version of the Bible isn't for four-year-olds, but there are plenty of books that are. I cut my reading teeth on books like *The Children's Story Bible* (The Grolier Society Inc., 1948), *Child's Bible Reader* (The Southwestern Company of Nashville, Tennessee, 1962), and Ruth S. Gray's *God's Good Gifts* (Broadman Press of Nashville, Tennessee, 1952), books that continue to grace my bookshelves to this day, by the way.

If you want your children to read their Bibles when they are older, you must introduce them to the fascinating stories and absolute truths found within the pages when they are younger. As they become older, teach them to turn to the Scriptures for the answers to their questions. Teach them early on that there is not one single issue God has not addressed within his Word.

GIVING YOUR CHILDREN THE GIFT OF YOUR ATTENTION TOWARD COMPANIONS AND ACTIVITIES

It has amazed me, in my interviews with youth, the number who have expressed this line or something close to it as their advice to parents: "Spend time with your kids. Know whom they hang out with, who their friends are, where they are going. Your time and attention are among of the greatest gifts you can bestow on them."

When we were in the beginning phase of our most difficult days with Jessica, my brother—a prodigal in his own right—gave me an invaluable piece of advice. "When her friends stop having faces," he said, "you're in trouble." It is imperative (I learned the hard way) to know (to the best of your ability) those whom your children call "companions" or "friends." With the media doing their levelheaded best to pull your children into dark places, you must be willing to work even harder to keep them in the light. When they were three, four, and five years of age you would never have thought of just letting them play anywhere or with whomever. You knew who their friends were. Don't stop keeping tabs on them just because they are now thirteen, fourteen, or fifteen.

This point leads me to another one: do be their parent; don't be their friend. At some point your relationship will change into more of a friendship, but you must know and understand where they need you to be in the equation. Friends they have; parents they need. Friends they can't always trust, but parents they should always be able to count on.

I remember when Jessica was little and she used to ask me for something and I would say no, and then she would reply, "I'll be your best friend." If the answer was still no, she learned that my role as a parent was more important to me than having her as my best friend. But, in time and as she matured, we began to use this expression as a sort of joke between us. "Mother, will you take me shopping? I'll be your best friend!" or "Jessica, will you go to see this movie with me? I'll be your best friend!" Now that she is an adult, our relationship has changed even again, and it is truly a beautiful thing. Gone is the teenager I often wanted to have exterminated. Here is a lovely adult woman of God whom I admire.

BEING AN IMAGE OF CHRIST IN THEIR LIVES

As an adult you cannot expect your children to be more like Jesus than you are or to walk more intimately with God than you do. Mom or Dad, if you are falling under the influence of the media—whether by way of music, television, movies, print, or the Internet—you truly have no right to expect anything different from your children. (This is not your turn to say, "But I'm an adult." Your role as an adult parent is to be an adult modeled after Christ first and foremost.)

BECOMING ACTIVE IN THEIR YOUTH ACTIVITIES

I am stunned at the number of youth pastors who tell me about the lack of parental activity within their church's youth programs. One pastor shared with me that when he called a parent just after having caught her child having sex during youth night within the church's building, he was met by an angry onslaught of words. "Why weren't you watching her better?" He calmly explained that, given the number of youth in the youth group, watching each individual was nearly impossible for him to do alone. "That's why I've incorporated a group of parents to come during youth activities and help us patrol to make sure our students aren't falling into temptation. If you'd like, I can add you to our roster of volunteers." The mother became even more adamant. "When I drop my daughter off at the church," she told the youth pastor, "she becomes your responsibility, not mine. This is my time to get some things done." Parent, as the mother of adult children, please let me assure you of one thing: your time will come. But, right now, your time must be invested in raising your children to the absolute best of your ability.

If your children don't appear eager to attend youth activities within the church, find out why. Youth groups can become cliquish. Ask your children why they aren't comfortable attending, be willing to listen, and don't take "I'm just not" as an answer. Not attending youth activities (or vacation Bible school, or Wee Worship, or Juniors for Jesus, or whatever your church offers) doesn't mean that you can't pour spiritual truths and knowledge into your children's lives. Form a small Bible study in your home. Take them out for special activities. Bottom line: get involved.

Recognize that your children are human beings and, just as you did in your youth, they struggle with very human emotions, tendencies, and temptations. We, all of us, are sexual beings. We, all of us, have natural desires toward sexual things. We, all of us, were made this way—and for a good reason. (Otherwise, there would be no people in the world.) However, just as you, as an adult, must curb your sexual appetites beyond what is expressly allowed within God's Word, so your children must control their sexual appetites. It is also critical to remember to teach your children the beauty of a sex life within the bounds of marriage and why what the media are doing often lessens such a gift from God.

In recognizing that your children are human, also recognize that they may make mistakes. In fact, in all probability, they will. When they do, and when they come to you seeking forgiveness and assistance in moving forward positively, don't "rake them over the coals." You are an example of God the Father. No matter how many times we, as adults, get it wrong, the Lord God still opens his arms to us and says, "I forgive you. I love you. You are still my child." God's mercies are renewed every morning, and so should yours be.

Ask your children's pastors what you should be looking for—the positives and negatives—when it comes to spiritual growth versus apathy toward God. I spoke to my friends Steven James ("The Story Guy," who writes to both kids and teens) and Sean Dunn (founder and director of Champion Ministries), asking what were some of the signs of apathy. Here is what they said.

"First of all," Steven began, "it's important not to go on a witch-hunt and get caught up judging people, but there are a few things to look for: Jesus gave a barometer of spiritual health in John 14:23–24, where he pointed out that those who love him will obey him, but those who do not love him will not obey him. So obedience and love for Jesus go hand in hand. If your teens have no desire to follow Jesus and no passion for doing what he says, then that lack of love will show itself by a lack of obedience and a pursuit instead for the things of this world. True devotion to Christ isn't simply expressed in words, but in actions. Regardless of how doctrinally precise our confessions might be, our lives are what truly reveal what we believe. So how do your children spend their time? Pursuing acclaim, popularity, and comfort, or are they more interested in serving Jesus and following him—wherever that might lead? How important is worship to them? (This is a good time for parents to read body language.) When you discover they have disobeyed Jesus, what's their response? Are they willing to change their ways, or are they more interested in excuses and evading the issue?"

"Kids who are apathetic," Sean adds, "tend to be self-righteous; have critical attitudes (especially toward spiritual leaders); would rather make excuses for their spiritual condition than take responsibility; have time for everything they want to do, but never find time to invest in their spiritual life; seclude themselves; and have weak convictions pertaining to morality."

PREPARING THEM REALISTICALLY FOR THE REAL WORLD

As shocked as I am by parents who raise their children willy-nilly, I am even more surprised—no, make that heartbroken—by parents who do not prepare their children for the realities of life. Recently, I was speaking with spiritual leaders within a small community about this very subject. "If we raise our children in a bubble," one woman said, "then when they float out into the world ... say, when they go to college, or out to get a job ... and those little bubbles pop, they'll come crashing down to the earth in a splat!" For this very reason, I don't believe we can shelter our children (I am not advocating absolute exposure either!), but we must instruct them from the time they are tots to make positive choices among the negatives possibili-

God is more powerful than any current of culture.

—Steven James[4]

ties. Even the viewing of some childhood cartoons can be harmful to spiritual growth. If you look closely—pay attention to the smallest details of their lives—you will find plenty of opportunities to educate and strengthen.

MY FINAL WORD: EVA MARIE

In the later part of the 1990s, Hilary Clinton quoted an old African proverb in a speech. She said, "It takes a village to raise a child." It does not take a village. It takes a parent. True, it is a blessing to have family, friends, and church family to help, but one strong parent willing to truly parent his or her children will be the hope of our future.

In a recent issue of *Pulpit Helps*, Taylor Dockery wrote, "To me the most widespread and devastating problem this country faces is immorality. Until we do something to change our ethics as individuals, our country as a whole will continue to suffer."[5]

Taylor Dockery is thirteen years old.

That said, we are also not without a great deal of promise for future generations.

MY FINAL WORD: JESSICA

I cannot tell you all the things America's youth is going through; I don't have the space, and I don't even presume to know them all. And it is different for every kid anyway. That's why you as a parent will have to ask your children to find out what their challenges are and what things are on their minds. Try having a conversation with your children or teens in which all you do is ask questions (you may have to ask more than once sometimes) and they do all the talking. Of course there will be things they may not feel comfortable talking about at first, and some will just take a little more time (for these things you will just have to try to imagine yourself in their shoes). Sometimes they may just need you not to give up too soon. Other times, it may just take them a few minutes to get started. In any case, it is important to remember that with young people, as with adults, timing is everything.

Over time, once the lines of communication have been strengthened and your children find you more and more approachable because of your nonjudgmental reception, you may find yourselves having a lot of "important talks" in which your kids are doing most of the talking, while your input is only a few lines at the end carefully designed and expressed to have an impact on them. If nothing else, at least try making them feel as though you are listening and are trying to understand, and be sensitive to "where they're coming from" before you give your perspective. You will be better received.

Remember that when you talk with your children or teens, it is important to keep in mind what you are trying to accomplish and not let emotions (or anything else for that matter) get you off track. If you are trying to connect with them and build a relationship with them in which your opinion is invited—or in the very least welcomed—the conversation is not going to be about who is right and who is wrong.

A mistake I have seen parents make is naively believing that if their children do something wrong, a negative influence was responsible. Kids need to learn to take control of themselves, and discipline is a must from an early age. I can't stress this point enough because it is much easier to learn discipline at age five than at age twenty-five, and in the end those youngsters who learn it will be the ones responsible for themselves. Every child is subject to temptation, and all children need help eliminating self-destructive behavior.

However, when your children do mess up, try to give them more than just the standard "do-and-don't" consequences of their actions. Meet them with some understanding and empathy. I say this because being too judgmental will make them feel that you may not be the best choice when they need help and guidance in the future, especially if they know that some of their decisions would not meet your standards for them. What if something bad happened to them at a party they knew they shouldn't have gone to, but they couldn't tell you for fear of your response to their even being in that situation? Or what if they do have sex and don't even tell you because they are afraid of your negative reaction? If that happens, you won't be able to help them with their struggles in that area. I know your fear could be that if you help them you will appear to be accepting their bad decision and saying it is okay (which I understand), but I don't think that necessarily has to be true. Either way, you should realize the risk you are taking by leaving them to look elsewhere for advice and information on some of the most crucial decisions they will make. Just remember when you talk to them that "all have sinned and fall short of the glory of God" (Rom. 3:23) and that "he who is without sin" should be the first to condemn others (John 8:7 NASB). Remember that even David messed up royally (pardon the pun), yet he remained God's child, found forgiveness, and was brought back to his keeping by the tie God had established with his heart from a young age.

As we know, in these days children are learning about very mature issues from an extremely young age. What is even scarier is the fact that no one can predict exactly which morsels

But, dear friends, remember what the apostles of our Lord Jesus Christ foretold. They said to you, "In the last times there will be scoffers who will follow their own ungodly desires." These are the men who divide you, who follow mere natural instincts and do not have the Spirit. But you, dear friends, build yourselves up in your most holy faith and pray in the Holy Spirit. Keep yourselves in God's love as you wait for the mercy of our Lord Jesus Christ to bring you to eternal life. Be merciful to those who doubt; snatch others from the fire and save them; to others show mercy, mixed with fear—hating even the clothing stained by corrupted flesh.

—Jude 17–23

of information they will receive on any given subject. If you want a real wake-up call, listen to kids "break down their take" on some very mature issues that they shouldn't even know exist, much less have a "take" on. For this reason you must stay well connected and start getting real honest with them from a much earlier age than you probably expected. There are a lot of adult issues that now exist in broad daylight for the world to see—some justified, some absolutely not—but all are being absorbed by our youth in the form of a lesson. That is just the way their minds work. They haven't been taught to be discreet in their words and actions, and no one can truly filter everything they see and hear. Regardless of the purpose of the message or the often figurative use of words that exists (in music for example), biological law says that its content must affect our youth in some way or another. And the existence of negative influences in the media is at an all-time high.

When your children come to you with tales of "everybody does it," whatever "it" is, you can be pretty sure that they are not that far from the truth. That is why they need to be daily reminded, "Do not be conformed" (Rom. 12:2 NASB), and "Your body is a temple" (1 Cor. 6:19). Remember that from their perspective it will seem that to choose to walk a separate path from the world and turn into "salmon that swim against the stream" will probably leave them alone and without a life.

Loneliness is a very underrated, yet overwhelming, fear for most teens. Don't let your children forget that their heavenly Father loves them more than they can imagine, so the things he says to protect them will not keep them from enjoying life, actually to the contrary. Keep them in the Word; have them attend church services weekly; and if they are a little older, help them find a church home where they are comfortable. Teach them how to be happy people and that true joy starts and ends with their relationship with the Most High.

POINTERS FROM JESSICA TO YOUR KIDS

- Regardless of what the world teaches, quick fixes are not the answer. Successful people believe in delayed gratification. Learn to apply this rule to all aspects of your life.
- Learn to search for the motivation behind every message you receive.
- You can appreciate an art form or an artist without wanting to become like him or her. In most cases the ones who live that lifestyle don't even want to do so, so why should you? That's not cool.
- It is a misconception that sex and love will prevent lonely, empty lives. You can never find or enjoy true love without first loving and respecting yourself enough to control your desires and emotions.
- Being yourself will make you happiest in the long run, not conforming. It is individuality that will make you attractive anyway, and eventually you will discover that you like the people better who like you for who you are. They will be less likely to have their own interests at heart.

- You cannot expect an output much different from your input.
- Sex is widespread not because it is the thing to do but because it is the way to make money. It is prostitution galore.
- Sex is not a mark of adulthood. It doesn't make you a grown-up, and you can be just as grown-up (if not more so) without it. It takes a lot of maturity to say no. That's something not everyone will tell you, and how can you expect them to do so when they couldn't even say no for themselves?
- A lot of the information you will receive about sex, especially from your peers, is based on myth. Find someone you can trust who represents what you want to become to discuss these things with.
- Keep yourself in the Word and never stop talking to God and listening to the Holy Spirit. These will be your only sources of strength in the hard times that I promise will come. Don't wait until you need God to build a relationship with him.

POINTERS FROM JESSICA TO PARENTS

- Counteract your children's negative input with positive input, and maintain the appropriate balance.
- Recognize that kids are often bored and need a purpose and goals. One of the best things you can do is help them develop an area of interest outside of school that is important to them (i.e., sports, work, drama, mission trips, whatever).
- Your kids want to share their life in general with you, so let them do so.
- There is good in the world even outside of the Christian market; be open to it.

- Face the fact that you can't keep your kids from all negative media; they can't even keep themselves from it.
- Kids are also thoughtful by nature, meaning that they consider a lot of things a lot of the time. Allow your children to draw their own conclusions about life and their place in it. You can help them adapt these conclusions later on in life.
- You are your kids' number one influence and role model, and that is much more than a right. It is a responsibility. Ask God to help you fulfill it to the best of your ability.
- Teach your kids responsibility by giving them a lot of it from an early age while you can still supervise them. Resist saving them from the consequences of their decisions. It will be easier on them learning discipline now rather than later.
- Make your kids feel comfortable to make mistakes as long as they never stop trying to do right and their hearts stay pure and their intentions holy.
- Understand that your kids may place you on a pedestal when they are young, but when they become preteens and teens, they may disrespect you. If they do, you may question their love, but if you hold on strong, when they start to get a taste of the real world, they will look back and realize all you were to them. If you are patient with them, they will end up respecting you above all others and will show you all the love you could hope for. You will become great friends. I promise. This is a cycle I have seen repeated with countless young people, including myself.
- Put your trust in your kids often for little things, and big things, even when they barely have faith in themselves. This confidence will teach them to trust themselves and

will give them enormous pride. It will also create a sort of accountability.

- Teach your kids to think for themselves even though you may at times disagree, as long as you both stay within the bounds of respect.
- Teach your kids how to have a relationship with God as their Father who will be there for them 101 percent every second of the day.
- Respect the fact that some times are better than others to talk to your kids about their life, and learn to recognize and take full advantage of the times when they want to talk.
- Believe that in your wildest dreams you don't know all your kids see and hear in a day, and probably never will.
- Don't be too naïve when it comes to your children. They are not immune to temptations no matter where they come from.
- Teach your kids to believe in delayed gratification in all aspects of their lives. "For who knows what is good for a man in life, during the few and meaningless days he passes through like a shadow?" (Eccl. 6:12).
- Don't be afraid of what you don't understand (or what you are intimidated by), because if you do so you will miss the opportunity to impart your wisdom and maturity and understanding into your kids' reality.
- Remember that if you don't answer your kids' questions, someone else will; and even if you do, they still will.
- Kids (even adults) can get caught up in their day-to-day battles and forget about the war that rages within them and outside them. Be aware of your children's struggles, and be patient with them while they work out their problems.

- Meet your children where they are without judging them and without sacrificing your own values or becoming weak and indulgent.
- Every child has a unique personality; the particular way he or she processes information, adapts to circumstances, and handles experiences is different. Respect these individual differences in your children.
- Learn to be creative with your kids so that they will understand and be positively affected by your lessons.
- Always empathize (i.e., listen carefully) before you emphasize (i.e., impart wisdom).
- Be honest with your children about the struggles and the difficulties they will face and are already facing. Share with them the realities of life so they won't be disheartened when they have no explanation for the things they see happening around them and to them.

In our world of mass media it's often difficult to escape the daily bombardment of information, but we do have the power to filter what we absorb. If we put good things in we can expect good results (think fiber).

—Christine Caine, A Life Unleashed[6]

- Give your children examples of some of the struggles and decisions in your own life. (Be honest with them and with yourself.) This will make you seem more human and more approachable.
- Remember that curiosity is as strong as peer pressure. Help your children learn how to direct their natural curiosity into the proper channels and away from sensuality and illicit sex.
- Introduce your children to new perspectives, and help

them find alternatives to negative, destructive patterns of behavior.

- Have faith in the foundation you gave your children to keep them grounded when you can't be there to protect them, even in the times when they stray from you and from God.
- Trust in God to protect your children, especially when they are far from you and him.
- Realize that it is a myth that increased knowledge of sexual subjects leads to greater chances of sexual experimentation and activity at a younger age. Studies continue to confirm this fact.
- Start having real conversations with your kids about sex very early on. Times have changed—children have questions at much younger ages now; and studies show that if children are already having sex, they are unlikely to stop based on new information they receive. You had better reach them first.
- If you see a lie in the media, be ready to explain it to your children.
- Since you can't really make your children do anything they don't want to do, you must help them find for themselves reasons to wait until marriage to have sex; otherwise, they probably won't. Messages of "just say no" leave little room for them to discover these gripping reasons and are no match for the media's "why not say yes?"

Real Talk with Real Parents

Part One

AT THE ROUND TABLE

Mike, 47 and his wife Debra, 43. They have two children, ages 11 and 12.

Bryan, 46. Father of seven children ranging in ages from 7 to 21.

David, 41 and his wife Robi, 42. They have two children, ages 13 and 16.

Amy, 40. Mother of three children ranging in ages from 8 to 15.

HOW DO YOU RESPOND TO YOUR CHILDREN WHEN THEY SAY, "I DON'T REALLY LISTEN TO THE LYRICS"?

Bryan: When I have concerns about the song titles that pop up, I look up the lyrics on the Internet. Because of the reputations of some artists, in some cases, I know right away that a problem exists. For example, I saw that one of my sons was listening to a song by Eminem. I looked up the lyrics and printed them out, though I hoped I wouldn't have to show the words to him. When I asked him about this particular song, he said that he doesn't really listen to the lyrics. He likes the rhythm and how the artist's words go along with the beat. I told him I understood that; I usually can't make out the lyrics myself, but I asked him if he knew that this song talked about ripping the genitals of young girls. He said he didn't, so I asked him to play the song in his mind and listen again. After looking up at the ceiling for a minute, he admitted that he could hear the words.

"You see," I explained, "if you can hear those lyrics in your head, they will affect you. You will be desensitized to obscenities and disgusting behavior. Not only that, you will be taking in messages from someone who proudly parades his hatred of good and worship of evil. Is this something you want to be associated with?" He shook his head and said, "You're right. It won't happen again."

The reason that I don't dress trashy is that I'm trying to set an example for little girls. From the time they're seven or eight years old, (girls) are being taught that the only thing that makes them special and beautiful is their sexuality, and I think that's wrong.

—Stacie Orrico, seventeen-year-old Christian recording artist[1]

Amy: I tell my children that everything they meditate upon becomes a part of them. Sometimes I'll start singing a song to myself that I knew years ago, then I'll realize the meaning of the words and wish so badly I could "flush" the song out of my mind. Because my parents were ignorant of the effects of negative music, my mind, like a computer, has hundreds of just bad songs filed away.

I remember the night I finally "gave in" to my boyfriend. Just a few minutes earlier, Rod Stewart's song "Tonight's the Night" came on the radio. "Don't say a word my virgin child, just let your inhibitions run wild." I didn't realize it then, but Satan literally coerced me with the words of that song. If I had been listening to a Christian radio station, I'm certain I wouldn't have made the same decision. Especially since I wanted so badly to save myself for marriage.

Robi: I say, "You know, I used to say that back in the day ... strange I can now sing the words to every song that was popular when I was a teen."

HOW DO YOU HELP YOUR CHILDREN MAKE POSITIVE CHOICES?

David: The best way is for them to see us make positive choices. The better a role model I am, and the better the choices I make, the better choices they will make. I also create an environment at home where they can ask me anything. Hopefully by doing that, they won't be afraid to ask for help. In the case of music, we do have some checks and balances though. They have to let us approve any CDs they purchase. We look at the lyrics together and then make a decision.

Robi: I don't like the WWJD [What Would Jesus Do]. What I do is talk to them about alternatives. In the Christian genre there are plenty of alternatives. We also have a rule with our boys. We read the lyrics before we buy a CD. If there is one F-word or the S-word, and so forth, then "No." But you also have to be careful when they burn CDs. The problem now is that you cannot tell if they downloaded legally or illegally. Legal downloads do not have any parental controls on the sites themselves as far as I know.

Real Talk with Real Parents

Part Two

STILL AT THE ROUND TABLE

Mike, 47 and his wife Debra, 43. They have two children, ages 11 and 12.

Bryan, 46. Father of seven children ranging in ages from 7 to 21.

David, 41 and his wife Robi, 42. They have two children, ages 13 and 16.

Amy, 40. Mother of three children ranging in ages from 8 to 15.

HOW DO YOU "CONTROL" WHAT YOUR CHILDREN SEE ON THE BIG SCREEN OR ON VIDEO?

Amy: Since I can't always be with them, I teach them that feeding on bad visual images and profanity pollutes minds. I arm them with information and help guide them to make good decisions. It's not about controlling my children; it's about guiding them.

Bryan: There are two basic rules. They are not allowed to watch any movie (theater) or video without permission. All movies not rated G must be screened by us, the parents, in one of two ways: 1. PG or PG-13 movies may be either viewed first by the parents or checked on a resource that is very thorough, like www.screenit.com

2. R rated movies will hardly ever be accepted, but on the rare occasions that an R movie seems that it may have edifying value (e.g. *The Patriot* or *The Passion of the Christ*), the parents will preview it. Checking it on screenit.com is not sufficient.

3. No NC-17 movies at all for any reason.

Robi: The movie and video decisions are all discussed. We have been very clear about what we do not want our boys to see and why. To back up our decisions we use Screenit.com and Pluggedin.com. Both sites give details about what's in a movie from a factual perspective rather than just an opinion. They list actual lines, count bad words, and spell out the violence and sexual content in plain factual language. I have overheard my kids say, "My mom checked it out on Screenit, and it has a bunch of sex stuff in it, and I don't really want to see that kind of stuff." It is almost like it shifts the blame to Screenit or the movie itself.

Debra: Our general rule is they can't watch PG-13 until they're thirteen, although we have let them on a case-by-case basis if we approve of it beforehand. R is not allowed until they're seventeen, and we try to teach them to choose their viewing wisely, and we don't watch many Rs because most of them aren't worth our time. We don't go to many movies or rent videos. We get most of our videos from the library, which we feel is better stewardship, so that helps us "control" what our children see.

How have you instructed your children to act if they
are at a friend's house and a movie is being shown that
you would not approve?

David: When they were younger, we set up a code word. If
something happened while they were at someone's house that
made them feel uncomfortable or was directly violating a family rule, they could ask to call home, and then they would mention the code phrase. Ours was, "Hey! I forgot that red ball I
wanted to bring over." That way our kids did not have to go
into detail in front of anyone about what was concerning them.
Then Robi or I would drop by the house and pick them up. It
only happened once, and it was because of a video. I just told
the parent I had forgotten about a family commitment we had
and that my son would not be able to stay over. Our boys are
now sixteen and fourteen, and at this age, we are encouraging
them to make the viewing decisions when they stay at a
friend's house. We have discussed with them what the options
are if a friend wants to watch or listen to something they know
they shouldn't. They believe the best line of defense in this situation is not to argue or condemn, but recommend alternatives.
These include, "Let's watch this instead of that," or "I brought
this movie to watch; why we don't watch this instead?" I have
overheard them making plans and asking questions about
movies, video games, and music over the phone before they go
to someone's house. I have also seen them take a movie of their
own, music of their own, and video games of their own. I think
that is smart. I am not sure I taught them that, but with older
teens especially it is a good plan.

Bryan: They're told that if they're comfortable with making an
objection, they should graciously tell them that they'd rather do
something else. We tell them it's okay to blame it on us. If
they're not comfortable with objecting, or their friends refuse to

have an alternative, they're to call us, and we'll come over and take them home.

Mike: They are to politely let the friend and parent know that they can't watch it.

WHAT KIND OF COMMUNICATION DO YOU HAVE IN PLACE BETWEEN YOURSELF AND OTHER PARENTS?

Bryan: We don't allow our children to go to homes without parents being present and telling the parents about our rules concerning entertainment. If a movie is suggested, our children know they are to call home and tell us what movie is going to be viewed. If we disapprove, they can request that another movie be considered or other entertainment be selected.

Robi: Our part as parents is to communicate with their friends' parents. We are responsible for knowing their views on movies and music. I make it a point to discuss TV, video, movies, the Internet, and music with other parents. I recognize that everyone has their own opinion, and once I know what another family approves or disapproves of, I know how to advise my kids when they plan to stay over.

HOW DO YOU RESPOND TO THE "BUT ALL MY FRIENDS HAVE SEEN IT; WHY CAN'T I?" QUESTION?

Mike: "We don't parent all your friends, only you." And then we discuss why we don't approve of it.

David: We started early being clear about what they could and could not see. When we say no, we show them what is concerning us, again by using Screenit or Pluggedin. Now they usually don't even come ask or complain. In addition they now feel like our decision to stand firm is helping other families take a closer look at their decisions, and I think they feel like they are helping their friends.

HOW HAVE YOU PREPARED YOUR CHILDREN FOR WHAT THEY MIGHT SEE IN THOSE "UNGUARDED" OR "UNEXPECTED" MOMENTS?

Robi: Honest communication is key. We make a big deal out of "being a virgin of the mind, body, and soul." We talk about what a challenge it is to remain a virgin of the mind and not just a physical virgin. But, you know, even the mall can be a danger zone. Victoria's Secret doesn't call us and warn us by saying, "Oh, by the way, the life-size picture in our window will be of a woman with no top on and very little panties." So things are going to happen whether by accident or in an unguarded moment or when a teen just makes a bad choice. All those will happen. We ask our sons how they are doing in the areas of quiet time, purity, honesty, and servanthood on a pretty regular basis. The purity question gets checked almost weekly and any time a situation comes up that warrants it. If we find out there has been any kind of incident, we talk about it. Forgiveness is included in that conversation, as well as preparing an action plan to deal with it in the future.

Debra: From little on, we have taught our children correct terminology for body parts, that sex is a gift from God for marriage, that marriage is between one man and one woman, that sex outside of marriage is sin. They know right from wrong, and they know many things they see in the media are wrong.

Bryan: We tell them that, over time, in their interactions with others, they'll see people doing things we don't approve of. So it's no huge surprise if they see something happen in a movie that violates our principles. What is to be done about it, however, is more difficult. If we are present, we can judge if what is being depicted is simply showing what evil people do with the hope that good will triumph. In those cases, we might allow the show to go on, unless we believe the scenes will create indelible impressions in their minds through the use of overly graphic images. If we are not present, we have told our children to leave the place of viewing (if possible) or turn their heads. We explain that sometimes violence is necessary for good to defeat evil, but if the movie is showing violence in gratuitous fashion (spurting blood, severed limbs, blades through the eye, and so forth.), then they should leave the room, if possible, or turn their heads. With sexual images, we offer no choice. They must leave, even calling us to come get them. I have yet to see the use of sexual images in a movie that can be considered acceptable.

HOW DO YOUR KIDS KNOW THEY CAN COME TO YOU WITH THEIR QUESTIONS?

David: You tell them ... over and over and over. It has to be supported by your daily interaction and interest in their lives with a healthy dose of hugs, pats on the back, sprinkled with little bits of surprise encouragement (email cards, note on the bed, favorite treat ...). Just saying it does not work.

Amy: I have never pretended to be perfect. My children understand that I have made and still do make mistakes. This makes it easier for them to come to me with their struggles. They know I will never judge them. We discuss Satan's schemes, his plans to lead us astray, and how we can avoid the pitfalls.

Mike: We've had open communication from birth. They know they can ask us anything, and believe me, they do! We're so glad they ask us instead of their friends, who may give them misinformation.

Bryan: Through practice from a very young age. We've told our children directly that they can tell us anything, even protesting our actions and commands, if they do so with civility and respect. We've outlined their boundaries carefully, and they have discovered that if they appeal with civility, they can sometimes get those boundaries stretched if the underlying principles are not violated. When we occasionally allow them to find a way to get what they want while clearly holding to our principles, they learn to trust that we are not hard-line ogres, but that we care both for their feelings as well as our values.

HAVE YOU EVER LET YOUR CHILD SEE A MOVIE YOU THOUGHT WOULD BE OKAY, ONLY TO DISCOVER IT WASN'T? IF SO, HOW DID YOU HANDLE IT?

Amy: Yes. My daughter and I walked out of the theater.

CAN YOU THINK OF ANY SPECIFIC TEACHABLE MOMENTS YOU'VE HAD WITH YOUR KIDS THAT RESULTED FROM WATCHING A MOVIE TOGETHER?

Bryan: Many times. Good movies allow wonderful times of discussion. In *The Lord of the Rings*, we talked about the unfailing loyalty of Sam, and [that] we should be that kind of friend for others. In *Mr. Smith Goes to Washington*, we talked about the pure integrity of Jeff Smith and his resolve to stand up for what was right in the face of seemingly unanimous opposition. In *The Patriot* we talked about the heroism of men and how they sacrificed for their families in order to preserve their freedom. We always take a little time after a movie to savor what we've seen, and those times have been precious.

David: Our family talks about everything, so there have been a bunch, but nothing specific comes to mind.

Christian Teens at the Round Table

[Note to parents: The teens we interviewed are sold-out Christians. Many of them are in leadership in one form or another. Their views are raw and real. They cut no corners with us as they spoke to us about what the world is like from their viewpoint and the influence of the media on their generation as well as the one that follows them. Some were interviewed by phone or via the Internet. Others met with us to share their views. The answers have been blended together for the reader's benefit.]

AT THE ROUND TABLE

Graham, 18	Barbara, 17
Sasha, 16	Lauren, 17
Abigail, 18	Kalyn, 17
Shayna, 16	Lisa, 17
DJ, 17	Sarah, 17
Nick, 16	Melanie, 18

WHEN I SAY "MEDIA," I'M TALKING ABOUT MUSIC, MOVIES, TV, MAGAZINES, AND THE INTERNET. WHAT AREA OF MEDIA HAS OR HAS HAD THE GREATEST INFLUENCE OVER YOUR LIFE?

Lauren: Music.

Melanie: Music.

Graham: Movies and TV.

Shayna: Internet and TV.

Barbara: Magazines, music, and TV.

Lisa: Music.

Sarah: TV. Because you get the most variety from it as far as categories go. Like music stars, movie stars, politics, news, and so forth.

Nick: Movies and music. A good CD or movie can change the way you look at the world.

DJ: Music.

HOW DIFFICULT IS IT FOR TEENS UNDER THE AGE OF SEVENTEEN TO ENTER AN R-RATED MOVIE?

[Lots of laughter]

Nick: If it's not *Passion of Christ*, not hard at all.

Lauren: Not at all.

Sasha: Not at all.

Barbara: How easy is it to get in? Most places check IDs, but all you have to do is get a ticket for another movie, and they don't check it when you go in.

Graham: It's pretty easy.

Melanie: It's not that hard. I have had people come up to me and ask [me] to buy their tickets for them, and if I wasn't a Christian and knew God wouldn't be happy with me, I would have bought them the ticket.

DJ: I know people who have done it, so it's probably easy.

Shayna: Very easy. Sometimes they'll check you at the door, and sometimes they won't. I've got in to four rated R movies, and I'm under the age of seventeen, and I wasn't asked to show ID.

Lauren: It's pretty easy.

Lisa: It's not hard at all.

WHAT IS YOUR FAVORITE TV SHOW?

Sasha: *Friends.*

Lisa: *Law and Order: SVU.*

Lauren: *Friends* and *CSI.*

HILARY BURTON, THE STAR OF *ONE TREE HILL*, SAID OF THE SHOW, "*ONE TREE HILL* IS VERY REALISTIC ... KIDS IN HIGH SCHOOL MAY SEE EACH OTHER NAKED FROM TIME TO TIME." HOW TRUE IS THAT LINE?

Barbara: Real true. Real, real, real true.

Sasha: Definitely, real true.

Barbara: Barbara says definite!

Shayna: I have to agree on that one.

Graham: That's pretty true, even on church trips.

DJ: I really can't say. I'm homeschooled, sheltered, and proud of it.

Melanie: I have never seen anyone naked, but going to a high school, it's probably more common than I give it credit for.

HOW DO SHOWS LIKE *WILL AND GRACE* OR EVEN *QUEER EYE* SHAPE YOUR VIEW OF HOMOSEXUALITY?

Melanie: I still think it's wrong, even though, I will admit, I have found *Will and Grace* hilarious.

Sasha: I think they're funny.

Lisa: They don't really. I find them amusing. My gay friends shape my view of homosexuality.

Barbara: They're cute! Not like they're hot or whatever, or I think they're attractive, but cute as in they're fun and they're entertaining.

Shayna: The shows or the gay people?

Barbara: Both.

Kalyn: I think it makes them easier to accept it [homosexuality] because it is cute, and then, you know, you'll like it.

Abby: Oh, yeah.

Graham: I think it makes the whole thing even weirder.

Barbara: Oh yeah, he's the boy. All the girls are like, "It's so cute!"

Shayna: For *Queer Eye* and *Will and Grace*, I don't really find that wrong, but that other show—*Boy Meets Boy*—that's disgusting.

Barbara: What's it about?

Shayna: It's like *The Bachelor*, but with only guys.

Barbara: Uh-uh! That's terrible!

Shayna: Little kids are watching that! I mean, what does that show kids now? Our generation knows that it's wrong, and that a boy and boy shouldn't be together, but my little sister who is three watched it one night.

Does sexuality really sell to the teen market?

Kalyn: Yes. Even with a bubblegum commercial.

Barbara: Yeah, the Orbit commercial or the Dentyne Ice … it's like, if you're naked, you're cool.

Nick: To the "average" teenager? Yes. To most people I hang out with? No. Because we understand that we are being sold to.

Melanie: Definitely, so many girls are caught up in trends and fads that they miss the whole picture.

Lisa: Yes, very much so.

Graham: Yes, it's the best marketing ploy to grab a guy's attention.

DJ: I'd say eight out of ten times.

How many hours a day are you online?

Lisa: Anywhere from one to three.

Graham: About two.
DJ: About one or two. Sometimes three.
Lauren: I'm calculating …
Melanie: Like one or two.
Nick: One or two, talking to my friends.
Abby: Not even an hour.
Kalyn: Two to three hours.
Sasha: Two-plus hours.
Lauren: . . . three or four.
Barbara: Two.

HOW MANY HOURS A DAY WOULD YOU SAY YOU SPEND IN QUALITY TIME WITH YOUR PARENTS?

Abby: Not even an hour.
Nick: I'd say about a half-hour to an hour.
Melanie: Maybe a half-hour. Sometimes not at all.
Kalyn: Never … especially on weekdays … on weekends if I don't have a soccer game or something going on … maybe an hour … or two at the most.
Graham: With my mom, a few hours. With my dad, none really.
Barbara: Probably like three hours a day with talking and dinner and all that. But probably more than if you would consider the "veg" time in front of the TV "quality" time.
Shayna: Not a lot of time. I get home and watch TV and most of the time fall asleep from like three-thirty to like six. My mom and I sometimes will spend some shopping time together, but not a lot.
DJ: About a year ago or so our family decided to do a crazy thing. We sold our house and bought a motor home. Up until just recently we've been traveling around the country, checking out all the things there were to see, and just enjoying family time. I think we grew much stronger over that time and learned to live with less and just enjoy each other.

HAVE YOU EVER BEEN "INVITED" TO A PORN SITE WHILE ONLINE?

Graham: All the time.
Barbara: Oh, hello! Only every five minutes!
Graham: Like those instant messages ...
Shayna: Yeah ... junk mail and yeah ...
Lisa: Yes.
Nick: Nope.
Sarah: Yes.
Melanie: Yes, and I happily declined. And one time, in the eighth grade, we were at a computer lab at school and asked to go to the Washington, D.C. Web site, and some kids typed it in wrong and got to a porn site.
DJ: Actually, yes; but it wasn't on my computer.

WHAT TYPES OF TECHNOLOGY DO YOU HAVE IN YOUR BEDROOM? OR DO YOU HAVE A COMPUTER IN A BACK ROOM OF THE HOUSE?

Melanie: A phone and a computer.
Graham: I have computers, TV, stereo.
Lisa: A stereo system with my computer being in a back room.
Barbara: How many computers, Graham?
Graham: Eight.
Sasha: Everything Graham said.
DJ: My brother and I have a computer in his room, but our parents have to put in a password for us to get on it.
Sarah: I have a computer.
Barbara: I have a computer in my room too.
Lauren: I do too.
Nick: I have a computer in the back room, not six feet from my bedroom. But in my room I have this big, awesome, retro-wood-paneled TV from like the eighties that's been in the family forever, an Xbox, a Super Nintendo, and a VCR.

Abby: Back room for me.

Kalyn: I have one in my TV room.

MEDIA SHOW TEENS TODAY IN "COMMON" SEXUAL SITUATIONS. BY "COMMON," I'M SAYING, "ORDINARY OR EXPECTED OR NORMAL." HOW REAL IS THAT?

Graham: Very real.

Lisa: It's very real. A large percent of kids I know are in those positions.

Sarah: Well, I think that a lot of couples today are having sex. A lot of the people I have talked to believe that you can have sex with whoever as long as you love them; no one cares about waiting until you are married anymore.

Barbara: I think it depends on the group. Our group it wouldn't be so normal, but in general, yeah, it's very common, normal, and accepted.

Abby: It's a pretty common thing when you've got kids in the bathroom at school having sex and in the parking lot. I mean, you can't even wait until you get home?

Graham: Kids are having sex in the [school's] bathroom.

Shayna: A couple of kids in my school have even been caught having sex in the classrooms after school.

Sasha: Ours too!

Barbara: Yes, it's very real!

Nick: Common to the point where it doesn't shock you, but you're still bothered.

IN YOUR OPINION, DOES MEDIA HAVE THE POWER TO SHAPE THE DECISIONS OF TEENS?

Abby: Yes.

Lisa: Yes.

Graham: Not fully. I believe it has a great impact on people, but I do believe that a lot of problems within the teenagers' decision about what they decide to do. It is more of a reassurance to teens that "everyone's doing it, and they seem to be fine, so why can't I?" or "Hey, it's cool to do that."

Sarah: Yes, I think it does.

Sasha: I think it has an influence, but I don't think [it] completely shapes us.

Melanie: A larger percent. People are losing home values and morals, so students have to go to other sources to find out how they are supposed to act and think.

Lauren: I think a lot of it has to do with that a lot of people are looking for answers, and if you don't have a strong foundation— whether it comes from home or a mentor or something—a lot of kids either do get their ideas from different people. A lot of it is the Internet, television, especially now that a lot of baby-sitters are televisions where you put it in your mind and in your heart, and it becomes who you are.

DJ: Yes and no. A lot of people base who they are on media, but not everyone.

In the book *Real Issues, Real Teens!* a teenage daughter tells her mother, "If you really want to know what teens are saying about sex, listen to the after-midnight [radio] broadcast." How would you respond to that statement?

Lisa: I'd say it's very accurate.

Shana: It's really sick. It's hard to find stations that don't have sexual talk or sexual lyrics. TV too. After midnight it's all adult situations.

Graham: I'd say it's pretty darn accurate. Especially as far as the crude sexual jesting goes.

DJ: They're nasty shows, but yeah a lot of teens talk about their sex life on them. I haven't ever heard an entire show or even more than like two minutes. I know a station that has a show called *Love Line.* That says it all.

Sarah: If you really want to know, just listen to MTV.

DO YOU THINK TEENS ARE MORE SEXUALLY ACTIVE TODAY THAN SAY TEN OR TWENTY YEARS AGO?

Nick: That's a tough question. There are many "Christian teens" who wouldn't think twice about having sex with someone; then there are the Christians who wouldn't go near it; then there are the believers in Christ who are in between—not afraid, but not tempted either.

Graham: Yes!

Melanie: Yes, definitely.

Lauren: Now it's more public.

Barbara: Now it's more cool, more popular.

Graham: Now if you don't do it, you're not accepted.

Sasha: Now it's more expected.

Graham: Now if you don't do it, you don't fit in.

Shana: Yeah.

Graham: Like, "You haven't had sex? Are you gay?"

Lauren: My mom will talk about it. She even told me that it went on in her school, but it wasn't talked about. They'd go to their little drive-in spots and get it on, but it wasn't talked about, but it was looked down upon. Now, it's a bragging right.

Barbara: I think it's definitely gotten much worse. Back then, families had more foundation, they were faith based even, and I think that created an environment where kids weren't ready to have sex at this age [because] they didn't want to have kids.

Graham: I think nowadays, the family is not the institution it used to be. Not that teenagers don't have the responsibility to do the right thing; it's just that a lot of kids are looking for answers, and what they see in media and celebrities who look [like] they're having a great time, and they ask themselves, "If it works for them, why doesn't it work for me?" And I believe that the media should be more responsible with what they put in the programs.

Barbara: So do I.

Abby: I think they're starting younger.

Kalyn: Yeah! So much younger! Like fifth graders.

Shayna: There's a girl in my biology class, she's thirteen years old, a freshman in high school, and she's eight and a half months pregnant.

Barbara: There're kids younger than that, dude! When I was a freshman in high school, I remember talking to my eighth-grade friends, and they're all, like, "We're having sex this weekend!" And I'm, like, I didn't hardly know what sex was when I was in middle school. I mean, I knew what it was, but that was about it.

Sasha: And, like, I haven't been involved in middle school at all since I left middle school, and to hear the things they hear every day and compare it to what we heard, it's like beyond belief.

Barbara: Yeah, it's gotten worse.

Sasha: One of my girls is telling me she's having trouble not being impacted by the group of friends she's with because they're all drinking and having sex and they're thirteen and fourteen. I'm sixteen, so that was only two years ago for me, and it's bizarre.

Kalyn: On the high school pregnancy thing, it starts even earlier than that. When I was in middle school, there was a girl on my bus who was in eighth grade who was pregnant. Now, every day after school I pick up a little girl from elementary school, and just the other day I'm watching the little boy flicking off every single car as he was walking by.

Shayna: I work with third graders in OJT (On the Job Training), and most of them know more cusswords than I do, and I'm in high school.

Barbara: It's funny to see which of those kids have older siblings. The older ones teach it to the younger ones.

Graham: Mmmm.

Lisa: To answer your original question, yes.

Sarah: More than ever.

WHAT ABOUT CHRISTIAN TEENS?

Graham: I'd have to say yes.

Melanie: Yes. Sometimes I believe it is easier for a Christian to give in to temptation than a non-Christian.

DJ: Yeah, sadly. I think a lot of Christian teens are part of the statistic. Mainly because we (as in Christian teens) let our guard down and don't expect it to happen to us.

Abby: I definitely do. In the past year I had three friends who got pregnant, and they're all Christians. Christian teens are definitely sexually active.

Barbara: I think Christian teens these days find it more accepting to be influenced by the media or to justify their lives or their sexual activity because of the media. They find it easier to bend the rules or to define "Christian" by their own standards and not by God's.

Sasha: I've been informed this year that I'm a pretty naïve person. The Christian friends that I've acquired have been mainly from my church and a few sporadic ones here and there, and in my Christian friend base, I say no. But then again, I don't know Christians who aren't so strong that they'd give in to something like that.

Lauren: How do you define "Christian" though? I can ask five people in a class, "Hey, are you a Christian?" and they say, "Yes," but they don't go to church—

Barbara: They don't have a personal relationship.

Lauren: They don't understand that just because they said the prayer at five years old ... so it depends on how you define Christian.

Barbara: Yeah, it depends on the personal relationship that determines what your standards are going to be.

Lauren: The people that I encounter that live the Christian life don't want anything to do with that, but the people who just say they are Christians, to them they might have that in the back of their mind, and they're able to excuse it. They say, "I'm not as bad as them if I do it."

Graham: Exactly. Media and Christianity can become really distorted. I went to a friend's church, and they were showing a sex scene from [a] movie. There was no real nudity, but it was a sex scene. And I said, "I can't believe you're showing that." And he says, "Oh, it's cool, man. Even my youth leader watches it." It's hard to believe. But so many boundaries have been knocked down. If one person accepts it, then someone else does. They're finding safety in numbers. When someone accepts it, then everyone else just believes it's okay. Morality has just dropped because of acceptance.

STATS TELL US THAT TODAY, TEENS—EVEN RELIGIOUS TEENS— HAVE DIFFICULTY DEFINING EXACTLY WHAT SEX IS. IS IT ONLY INTERCOURSE, OR DO OTHER FORMS OF SEX FALL INTO THAT CATEGORY?

Lisa: I consider only intercourse to be sex.

Graham: Other forms.

Melanie: Anything that has you taking your clothes off in front of the opposite sex I would consider sex. That's why I also get angry about fashion, because sex is not just physical but mental, and some guys can't control themselves around girls who don't know how to dress.

Nick: It varies from teen to teen. It comes back to the three levels: there are those who think that everything is sex; those who think that only things without the clothes are sex; then there are those who only think intercourse is sex. I go for the clothes idea.

Sasha: I've never really known the answer to this, so I'd be interested to hear—

Barbara: But do you think that's, like, God's way of telling us,

"Don't have sex before marriage"? Do you think he means inter-course or other forms of sex? That's a question that I have too.

Abby: It says in the Bible that we're to have no hint of sexual immorality in our lives. I think that any form of anything that crosses the boundaries is a hint of sexual immorality.

Barbara: Does that mean kissing?

Abby: No, I think it's like, where do you draw the line?

Graham: What your standard is. Obviously, the higher the stan-dard the better. I don't believe everything is wrong, but there is also a verse in the Bible that says just because something is not said in the Bible is wrong, it doesn't mean it's not. So there're other forms of sexuality that I didn't even know about until I heard some little "nose-blowers" talking about it.

Lauren: These days, kids are like, "I'm having oral sex, but it's not sex." I'm like, "It's not called oral kissing; it's called oral sex. Why do you not understand that that's just as demoralizing, and you're going into that foreign territory that you shouldn't even come close to?"

WHAT DO YOU KNOW ABOUT A AND F'S (ABERCROMBIE AND FITCH'S) MAG-ALOG?

Melanie: You might as well go and buy a porn magazine.

Lisa: It's really porn with a not-so-dirty name. I wouldn't buy it, but then again I really dislike A and F.

Lauren: I have a friend whose mom bought him one, and we're just looking through it. I mean, I swear, it was like pornography. I was like, "You're trying to sell me clothes, but I don't see any clothes."

Barbara: They're lying over there!

Lauren: I'm like, "That's a cute … um … top." It makes me uncomfortable.

Graham: They're totally taking advantage of the fact that sex does sell to our culture, and they use that, even though—like

Lauren said—there are not many clothes in their catalog. They're just totally taking advantage of that, knowing that guys especially have [a] sin nature to look at that. Like, "Wow, there's nudity in this magazine, so I'm going to get this one." So they get it, and it just gives [A and F] more money.

Abby: It's so easy to get it.

Shayna: After I saw the magazine—with every other page nude, a girl topless—I refuse now to shop there.

Barbara: Their clothes don't even fit me.

Shayna: I did shop at Abercrombie before they started using nudity to sell their clothes, but their skirts are getting shorter; their shirts are getting lower and tighter ...

Barbara: ... and a little more see through.

Shayna: I don't want to wear something just because it has a name on it.

Sasha: A girl yesterday was wearing an Abercrombie skirt in my anatomy class, and she walked in, but she wouldn't sit down. We were, like, "Why don't you sit down?" She was, like, "My skirt's too short."

Barbara: Eww! Why would you wear that?

Lauren: She stood in every single class?

Sasha: She stood in class. And if she didn't, she had to put something in her lap. She even stood through the whole lunch period. And I'm saying, "What an idiot. Why would you even wear that skirt?"

Barbara: Hey! You've already got us thinking, you might as well show it off.

GUYS, WHEN YOU SEE GIRLS WEARING SHORTS OR SWEATS WITH WORDS WRITTEN ACROSS THE BUTTOCKS, DO YOU LOOK?

Graham: I think it's retarded. It's like, "What is that saying ... um? 'Juicy'?" I find it offensive, because whenever they say something, your eyes automatically just go there. And then my eyes sin.

DJ: I'd say there is always that first look. On a personal basis I just try to ignore it, but you are always curious to what it says.

Nick: Yeah, but it's usually not worth the effort.

Barbara: It's frustrating. Even the little cheerleaders I coach, the practice uniforms they're given by Pop Warner say "Cheer" across the butt. Or even my basketball uniforms have "RAMS" across the butt. It's not necessary. You know? If you can drive past a billboard at sixty miles an hour and know what it says, you can drive past someone's butt and know it says "Cheer" too.

HOW BIG A DEAL IS SEX BEFORE MARRIAGE REALLY?

Barbara: Huge!

Graham: Yeah.

DJ: Big deal for me. I'm waiting till I get married. God will bless that, and that is something worth blessing.

Lisa: It's a big deal as far as consequences and results, but I think it's not as big of a deal as people say. It won't condemn or save your soul. You either do it, or you don't.

Melanie: Huge! My parents had sex before marriage, and that is why they got married, because my mom got pregnant with my oldest sister. And I can tell you, it's hard having parents who didn't marry for love. And seeing so much divorce scares me.

Barbara: I don't want my husband to have had any sexual encounter. Like, I want to be his first kiss. I'm sorry, but what if he's kissing me and thinking about some other girl, thinking, "Man, my other girlfriend was a better kisser."

Graham: I've always been worried about comparison; I'd never want my wife to experience anything outside of marriage because I wouldn't want her to think, "Oh, Graham is nothing compared to this other guy!"

Barbara: [Laughing] Oh, Graham, you're everything!

[Laughter]

Lauren: [Sobers] Um, in the group in here it's huge, but you could go to school and—

Barbara: —it's huge all right because we're doing it all the time—

Lauren: It's not an option anymore. Not even a thought process. Because, even though nowadays people are waiting longer to get married, the thought of not having sex until I'm thirty? That can't happen. So, in some cases it's a big deal and something of value and in other cases—

Shayna: Sex before marriage: I think that as long as you don't keep it from your husband—if I tell him about having sex before marriage and that I regretted doing it—I think you should be forgiven for it now that you're with him and only him.

Barbara: Yeah, but some people think that if they did it before they were a Christian, and now they are, and they've been redeemed, they can just keep on doing it. I think that's absurd.

Graham: It's not even a matter of forgiveness though. Like, if my wife had sex before marriage, I would forgive her, but still there would be … it would feel like … some sort of division. And if I knew that she'd gone out there and had sex by her own choice, that would hurt me.

Nick: To me it's everything. I believe completely and totally in spiritual sex and love my wife too much to cheat on her before I know her.

Kalyn: I'm in AP [Advanced Placement] psychology this year, and our teacher likes to do a lot of surveys. One of the surveys had a list of drugs, and sex was one of the things on the list. He had us write down on a piece of paper whether or not we did it. Usually the AP students have a higher standard, but over 60 to 70 percent of the AP students had had sex.

Sasha: A couple of my friends I've been talking to lately, we got into that conversation on Sunday, actually, and I was the only virgin in the room. One of the girls was like, "My first time was just with a friend because I didn't want it to be anything big or serious."

Barbara: They want to just get it out of the way.

Lauren: I have some friends who've told me they have, and I'm like, "Really? You?"

(Laughter)

HOW DO YOU FEEL ABOUT [REALITY] SHOWS LIKE *THE BACHELOR, EXTREME DATING, ELIMIDATE, FIFTH WHEEL, REAL WORLD?*

Graham: *Fifth Wheel* is awesome. But I think they're incredibly obscene.

Sasha: Sasha thinks they are so dumb!

Barbara: I like them!

DJ: I think they are so far from reality it's hilarious. Just stupid. A guy could never be with that many beautiful women.

Abby: I think they're hilarious!

Nick: I think they're hilariously bad and watch them to laugh at them, but I can only take so much.

Barbara: It's fun to make fun of the people. They're so low class.

Kalyn: It is funny, but like how stupid can you be to think you're going to fall in love in a week?

Shayna: I have to agree with Kalyn. I don't really watch them, but if you want a laugh, then, yeah, watch them.

Lisa: Reality TV is stupid. They all suck.

IF YOU COULD TELL PARENTS ONE THING YOU THINK THEY SHOULD KNOW BUT THEY PROBABLY DON'T KNOW, WHAT WOULD IT BE?

Lisa: More kids are smoking pot than you think.

Sarah: I think that they should know a lot of teens know more than they should about a lot of things regarding sex and drugs. It's sad but true.

Kalyn: I would tell parents not to be as trusting as they are toward their kids.

Graham: Yeah, not to have the kind of trust level that they do.

Lauren: Once they [children] freaking know they have your trust, they can get away with anything.

Graham: Yeah, also I don't want my parents to be overbearing, but I also have a Christian foundation. Some kids don't have that. Some parents are just too lenient, not playing a role in their kids' lives, ignoring what they do after school. Then a lot of kids will see that as a form of entertainment and will escape to that. My parents have been pretty strict on me, but I've really appreciated that because there's no telling what that saved me from.

Abby: I value my dad's trust more than anything. It's something that I fight to keep and makes me really sad when we start to lose it. I think a parent trusting their kids and letting them know that they have the trust is ever so important.

Lauren: I think a lot of parents have blinders on. "My kid would never do that." A lot of parents are very naïve. Your kids are dealing with a lot more than you realize. Leave the lines open for your kid to come to you. There has to be a line of communication. But don't be stupid. Don't think, "Oh, my child would never do that," and as you're saying it, they're sneaking out the door to go to a party and get drunk.

Barbara: To Christian parents I would say, "Help your kids grow in their faith." See what you have, but don't take it for granted. You have no idea how hard it is to be a Christian kid these days, to maintain your faith. Appreciate it. Reward them. Keep being just as strict. To the non-Christian parent, to any parent: Kids can fake character.

Kalyn: My mom trusts me, and I don't know why. When I was younger, she was working, and I would stay with friends, and she had no idea what I was doing.

Barbara: Parents have blind trust until their kids give them a reason not to.

Graham: They want to be in denial. If parents would just accept the fact that their kids may not be perfect ...

Abby: If I could say something to parents it would be this: Actually listen to your kids. Don't try to offer solutions; just listen. And you need to educate yourselves and then give them a good reason not to do certain things. Don't just say talk them out of it, but give [them] a good reason. Spend time with them really.

Shayna: I never really got the sex talk. I learned about it all from school. I'm more open with my friends' parents than my own parents.

Barbara: Parents need to understand that just because your kids are not talking to you, it doesn't mean that they aren't talking to someone else, but it also means they should be able to talk to you.

Shayna: Yeah, like, I go to my parents to talk, and they're like, "Oh, we'll talk later, honey," while they're staring at television for four hours. If your kid is ready to talk, stop what you are doing, and listen to them.

Graham: Yeah. Set that time aside. Don't watch TV, but spend time with your kids.

Sasha: And don't freak out when we tell you something. Don't overreact. Be supportive. Don't break down crying. That's only going to make us back away.

Graham: Exactly. What's happened has happened. Deal with what you've got.

Lauren: Some parents are just up and down. They have strong boundaries in some areas, and they're weak in others. They're not consistent. The kids are grounded, but they can do this and that throughout the week. Be consistent.

Melanie: I'd tell them that they need to learn to be better parents.

Seriously, I mentor middle schoolers, and most of their problems are with their parents. Most of my problems are with my parents. Expecting too much, or just not caring. Parents are human, I understand, but I know when I become a parent, I won't have my life anymore. It will become my children's. All of my time will be put into them. I think parents nowadays get so caught up in their own things that they neglect their children.

Barbara: If you expect something out of your kids, then set the example. We should mirror you, so set the example.

DO TEENS REALLY LISTEN TO THE LYRICS OF MUSIC OR NOT?

Lisa: Yes, we do.
Graham: Yes.
Barbara: Yes.
Graham: I was coaching for an elementary school, and they were singing the lyrics from 50 Cent and stuff. I'm like, "How do you guys know this stuff? You guys are in elementary school, and you know, like, every word!"

WHO SINGS THESE LYRICS: "THE CONVERSATION GOT HEAVY, SHE HAD ME FEELING LIKE SHE'S READY TO BLOW"? [AUTHORS' NOTE: THESE LYRICS ARE FROM "YEAH" BY USHER.]

[Teens begin to sing the song: "She saying, 'Come get me' so I got up and followed her to the floor."]

Barbara: Yeah! Yeah, like we've never heard that song before.
Lauren: I learned that on Road Rules. *[Authors' note: Road Rules is a church-sponsored senior class trip.]*
Sasha: Yeah! "Take that, rewind it back."[1]
Nick: Sex, sex, and more sex.

WHEN YOU HEAR THOSE LYRICS, WHAT PICTURE COMES TO
YOUR MIND?

Lisa: They make me think of sex.

DJ: Ummm, sexual stuff, nasty dancing, not like nasty—nasty but dancing that has sexual moves and stuff.

Abby: I never thought about it.

Sasha: I was thinking about this the other day, "She's got me feeling like she's ready to blow"? I just don't get it.

Lauren: Ask your mom, Sash!

Notes

INTRODUCTION

1. Eva Marie Everson, *Shadow of Dreams* (Uhrichsville, OH: Barbour, 1997), *Summon the Shadows* (Uhrichsville, OH: Barbour, 2002), and *Shadows of Light* (Uhrichsville, OH: Barbour, 2003).

2. Jack Samad, *Sex and Young America*. From the National Coalition for the Protection of Children and Families: *Sex and Young America* is a unique relationship-driven tool that helps educate, challenge, and encourage young people in their decisions about sexual activity and its consequences. The entire package, a combination of videos and written curriculum for use in youth group settings, also serves as a conversation starter for meetings with youth and will give parents an idea of what will be discussed with their children.

3. Pamela Kruger, "Are the Media to Blame ... or Not?" *Child*, October 2003, 40.

4. For more information about the Magdalene Project or how to incorporate a satellite ministry in your area, contact Robbi Sluder at 512-292-1108, The Magdalene Project, Intl., P. O. Box 151058, Austin, TX 78715. http://www.themagdaleneproject.org/

5. Chris Russell, media specialist at Orangewood Presbyterian Church, Maitland, FL, personal interview, August 2004

6. Vicki Courtney, *Your Girl* (Nashville: Broadman and Holman, 2004), 4.

7. Barna Research Online, "Teenagers,"
   http://www.barna.org/FlexPage.aspx?Page=Topic&TopicID
   =37.

8. Dr. Ted Baehr in discussion with the author, June 2004.

CHAPTER 1

1. MTV Web site, "Fight for Your Rights: Protect Yourself,"
   http://www.mtv.com/onair/ffyr/protect.

2. Mary Webb, email message to author, January 2004.

3. Barna Research Online, "Teenagers,"
   http://www.barna.org/FlexPage.aspx?Page=Topic&TopicID
   =37.

4. American Academy of Pediatrics Committee on Public
   Education, "Sexuality, Contraception, and the Media,"
   Pediatrics 107, No. 1 (2001),
   http://www.aap.org/policy/re0038.html.

5. Focus on the Family, *Family News in Focus*, March 10, 2004:
   www.family.org.

6 American Academy of Pediatrics Committee on Public
   Education, "Sexuality, Contraception, and the Media,"
   Pediatrics 107, No. 1, (2001),
   http://www.aap.org/policy/re0038.html.

7. Scott Covington and Curt Swindoll, "Pornography: No
   Longer a Dirty Little Secret," Crosswalk.com:
   http://www.crosswalk.com/faith/1224639.html.

8. G. W. (Bill) Reynolds III, *Sin City* (Jacksonville, FL: River
   City Press, 2003), 20.

CHAPTER 2

1. "Online NewsHour: Indecency On the Air," February 11,
   2004; A NewsHour with Jim Lehrer Transcript; Online Focus
   (http://www.pbs.org/newshour/bb/media/
   jan-june04/indecency_02-11.html).

2. Lewis Grizzard, *An Evening with Lewis Grizzard*, DVD, (1986; New York, NY: BMG Special Products, 2001).

3. Associated Press, "Former N'Sync Member Bashes Standards Hype," http://music.yahoo.com/read/news/12176578, March 1, 2004.

4. World of Celebrities, "Britney Spears," www.world-of-celebrities.com/britney_spears/

5. "Is It True?" *In Touch*, March 1, 2004, 32.

6. Kevin Chappell, "Mary J. Blige's Tearful Plea: I've Got to Be Me," *Ebony*, October 2003, 42.

7. Eminem, "My Dad's Gone Crazy," *The Eminem Show*, May 26, 2002, Interscope Records.

8. Eminem, "My Dad's Gone Crazy."

9. *Live! with Regis and Kelly*, March 3, 2004.

10. Phil Chalmers in discussion with the author, February 2004.

11. *True Lies*, "The Four Lies," http://www.truelies.org/four_lies.html.

12. Cynthia Davis, *YS* magazine, February 2004, 8.

13. *High Fidelity*, directed by Stephen Frears, (Burbank, CA; DVD, video, Touchstone Pictures, 2001).

14. Walt Mueller, *More Than Noise*, VHS video (2002; Elisabethtown, PA: Center for Parent/Youth Understanding).

15. Walt Mueller, *Understanding Today's Youth Culture* (Wheaton, IL: Tyndale, 1999).

16. Walt Mueller, *how to use your HEAD to guard your heart*, Center for Parent/Youth Understanding (Elizabethtown, PA).

17. Mueller, *More Than Noise*.

18. Mueller, *More Than Noise*.

CHAPTER 3

1. According to *The Godly Business Woman Magazine*'s Web site (and data taken from the Consumer Women's Network), 66 percent of women work full time, 73 percent of married

mothers of children under eighteen are in the workforce, and 91 percent of single mothers work. Of major concern: finding affordable childcare.

2. Newton N. Minow and Craig L. LaMay, *Abandoned in the Wasteland* (New York: Hill and Wang, 1995, 1997), 17.

3. Minow and LaMay, *Abandoned in the Wasteland*, 5.

4. James P. Steyer, *The Other Parent* (New York: Atria Books, 2002), 11.

5. Wikipedia, The Free Encyclopedia, "I Love Lucy," http://en.wikipedia.org/wiki/I_Love_Lucy

6. Mediascope, "Teens, Sex, and the Media," http://www.mediascope.org/pubs/ibriefs/tsm.htm.

7. Minow and LaMay, *Abandoned in the Wasteland*, 3.

8. http://en.wikipedia.org/wiki/I_Love_Lucy

9. Music News, November 2003, "Madonna Bans TV." www.platinum-celebs.com/music/news/2003_11_13.html.

10. Minow and LaMay, *Abandoned in the Wasteland*, 10–11.

11. Penn, Schoen and Berland Associates and American Viewpoint, "The 2003 Common Sense Media Poll of American Parents," May 2003, 9: http://www.commonsensemedia.org/about/press/Parents pollMay212003.ppt, June 6, 2003.

12. Kaiser Family Foundation, *Kids and Media @ the New Millennium* (Menlo Park, CA: Kaiser Family Foundation, 1999), 15.

13. J. Peterson, K. Moore, and F. Furstenberg, "Television viewing and early initiation of sexual intercourse: Is there a link?" *Journal of Homosexuality*, Vol. 21, 1991, 93–118.

14. Stacy L. Smith and Ed Donnerstein, "The Problem of Exposure," taken from *Kid Stuff*, Diane Ravitch and Joseph P. Viteritti (eds.) (Baltimore: The Johns Hopkins University Press, 2003), 71.

15. TV Tome, "Sex and the City," www.tvtome.com/SexandtheCity/

16. HBO.com, "Deadwood," http://www.hbo.com/ deadwood/?ntrack_para1=leftnav_category0_show3.
17. Teen Health and the Media, "Media Literacy; Fast Facts," http://depts.washington.edu/thmedia/view.cgi?section= medialiteracy&page=fastfacts.
18. While these are the shows featured on network television, they are not reflective of cable shows such as *The Sopranos* and *The Commish*, which are, in the author's opinion, most definitely for mature/adult viewing.
19. Internet Movie Database (imdb.com), "Plot Summary for the *Phil Donahue Show*," http://imdb.com/title/tt0065335/plotsummary.
20. Bernard M. Timberg, "Talk Shows" The Museum of Broadcast Communications: http://www.museum.tv/archives/ etv/T/htmlT/talkshows/talkshows.htm (April 19, 2005).
21. Scott, *Can We Talk?*, 225.
22. Scott, *Can We Talk?*, 228.
23. Senator Joseph Lieberman, "Why Parents Hate TV," *Policy Review*, May–June 1996, http://www.policyreview.org/may96/lieber.html.
24. *The Oxford American Dictionary of Current English* (New York: Oxford University Press, 2002, 260.
25. *The Washington Times* (Washington, D.C.), April 2, 2004: washingtontimes.com.
26. Alessandra Stanley, "The Ancient Days of Teenage Drama," *New York Times* (New York), April 2, 2004: nytimes.com.
27. Alessandra Stanley, "The Ancient Days of Teenage Drama."
28. The WB Web site, "*One Tree Hill*," http://www.thewb.com/ Shows/Show/A/0,7353,| |1490~1,00.html.
29. Hilarie Burton, who plays Peyton Sawyer on the WB's *One Tree Hill*, as quoted in "Random Rants, 2004. The WB Television Network: http://www.thewb.com/ Popups/Video/0,8204,139117,00.html

30. About.com, "TV/Movies for Teens":
http://teentvmovies.about.com/library/bl7heavendesc.htm.

31. Joel Federman,"Rating Sex and Violence in the Media:
Media Ratings and Proposals for Reform," A Kaiser Family
Foundation Report, November 2002.

32. Barbara Hattemer and Robert Showers, *Don't Touch That
Dial* (Lafayette, LA: Huntington House Publishers, 1993).

33. Hattemer and Showers, *Don't Touch That Dial*

34. Chuck Gartman, "Helping Teens Deal with Their Sexuality,"
Living with Teenagers magazine, Vol. 25, No. 2, August 2003, 8.

35. Steyer, *The Other Parent*, 184.

36. Scott McCurdy in an email to the author, January 2004.

37. Steyer, *The Other Parent*, 199.

38. University of Missouri, Kansas City, "Teens and Sex":
www.umkc.edu/sites/hsw/teens/index2.html

39. University of Missouri, Kansas City, "Sex in the Media":
http://www.umkc.edu/sites/hsw/other/sexmedia.html.

CHAPTER 4

1. Gerald Mast, *A Short History of the Movies*, 4th Edition (New
York: Macmillan Publishing Co., 1986), 5.

2. Tom Dirks, "Film History of the 1920's":
http://www.filmsite.org/20sintro.html.

3. Carla Donnell, "Mini Biography of Mae West," IMDB.com.

4. Nell Minow, *The Movie Mom's Guide to Family Movies* (New
York: Avon Books, 1999), 25.

5. Taken from World Book Online "Hippies":
http://www.aolsvc.worldbook.aol.com/wb/Article?id=ar25
7510.

6. Ted Baehr, *Movieguide Best 2003 Films for Families/Best 2003
Films for Mature Audiences*, Vol. XIX, 5/6, March 2004, 28.

7. William D. Romanowski, *Pop Culture Wars* (Downers Grove,
IL: InterVarsity Press, 1996), 35.

8. Claudia D. Johnson, "That Guilty Third Tier: Prostitution in Nineteenth-century American Theaters," *Victorian America*, Daniel Walker Howe (ed.) (Philadelphia: University of Pennsylvania Press, 1976), 118.

9. Robert P. Lockwood, *Our Sunday Visitor*, April 12, 1996.

10. Motion Picture Association of America, "About MPAA/MPA": http://www.mpaa.org/about/index.htm.

11. Michael Medved, *Hollywood vs. America* (New York: HarperCollins/Zondervan, 1992), 181.

12. Ted Baehr, *The Media-Wise Family* (Colorado Springs, CO: Chariot Victor Publishing, 1998), 151.

13. Baehr, *The Media-Wise Family*, 151.

14. Nell Minow, *The Movie Mom's Guide to Family Movies*, 25.

15. Baehr, *The Media-Wise Family*, 152.

16. Taken from http://www.cpyu.org/pageview.asp?PageID=8696.

17. Teenage Research Unlimited is the nation's foremost market researcher specializing in the teen market. It can be found at http://www.teenresearch.com/home.cfm.

18. Information gathered from the *Merriam-Webster Online Dictionary*; also Michael Shields, "Publishers Eye Teen Market, Find Explosive Growth; Diversity; Optimism," *Media Daily News*, June 22, 2004.

19. Romanowski, Pop Culture Wars, 30.

20. A movie stuntman on films such as *Lethal Weapon 4* and *Blade*, James Sang Li is also a youth pastor in the Orlando, Florida, area.

21. In 2003 RS Entertainment released a movie about the life of Martin Luther, *Luther*, which was met by excellent reviews. In 2004, *The Passion of the Christ*, a movie about the twelve hours leading up to the crucifixion of Jesus, drew an unbelievable amount of press and fanfare. Mel Gibson literally put his career and his money "on the line," as Mr. Li said it. "Producers," Li said, "make movies to make money … not spend it."

22. *The Graduate* (MGM/UA, 1967).
23. Ted Baehr, "The Ratings Game," *The Media-Wise Family* (Colorado Springs: Chariot Victor Publishing, 1998), 155.
24. *Scary Movie 3* (Miramax Home Entertainment, 2003) (along with the Coors Beer Company) came under fire by the Marin Institute when the Coors Twins were featured in this teen-targeted movie.
25. *Dodgeball* (Fox Home Entertainment, 2004) (along with Anheuser-Busch) came under fire by the Marin Institute because of the blatant PR-ing of Bud and Bud Light in this teen-targeted movie.
26. Baehr, *The Media-Wise Family*, 148.
27. Michael Medved, "Want an Oscar? An 'R' Revs Up Your Chances," *USA Today*, Thursday, March 18, 1999.
28. Nell Minow, *The Movie Mom's Guide to Family Movies*, 6.
29. Nell Minow, *The Movie Mom's Guide to Family Movies*, 3.
30. Nell Minow, *The Movie Mom's Guide to Family Movies*, 7.
31. Jessica Weiner is the author of *A Very Hungry Girl* (Hay House, 2003); a popular guest expert on CNN, MTV, *The Oprah Winfrey Show*, *The View*, and *Good Morning America*; and is considered an actionist, which is someone who motivates and inspires people to take action in their everyday lives.

CHAPTER 5

1. Reported by Harlan Schwarz, supervisor of advertising and marketing, MPA. Harlan Schwarz, *Media Daily News*, June 22, 2004.
2. Reported by Harlan Schwarz, supervisor of advertising and marketing, MPA.
3. Michael Shields, "Publishers Eye Teen Market, Find Explosive Growth, Diversity, Optimism," *Media Daily News*, Tuesday, June 22, 2004.

4. Michael Shields, "Magazine Spotlight: *YM*," *MediaDaily News*, Monday, July 12, 2004.

5. Each year, teenage girls spend more than $4 billion on cosmetics. J. Brown et al. "Mass Media, Sex and Sexuality," *Adolescent Medicine: State of the Art Reviews*, Vol. 4, No. 3, October 1993.

6. One of the April 2004 cover articles in *YM* (Your Magazine) was "Does Your Life Suck? We'll Fix That."

7. Mara Reinstein, "Britney and Madonna New Best Friends," *Us* magazine, September 15, 2003.

8. Or "10 Thrilling New Mattress Maneuvers."

9. Courtney, *Your Girl*, 4.

10. "Virginity, Why All the Hype?" *Teen Voices*, Vol. 11, Issue 2.

11. Melissa Daly, "Let's Talk about Sex," *Seventeen*, July 2003.

12. "Ask Ryan," *Guideposts Sweet 16*, Vol. VI, No. 6, August/September 2004, 41.

13. Referenced in Sheila Gibbons, "Teen Magazines Send Girls All the Wrong Messages," Women's E-news, October 19, 2003. http://www.womensenews.org/article.cfm/dyn/aid/1580.

14. Gibbons, "Teen Magazines Send Girls All the Wrong Messages," Women's E-news, October 29, 2003

15. Leilani Corpus, "What We've Learned from Ted Bundy": http://www.forerunner.com/forerunner/X0332_Ted_Bundy.html.

16. Rotten.com, "Ted Bundy," http://www.rotten.com/library/bio/crime/serial-killers/ted-bundy/.

17. Bryan Davis, *Spit and Polish for Husbands: Becoming Your Wife's Knight in Shining Armor* (Chattanooga, Tenn.: AMG Publishers, 2004), 168.

18. Davis, *Spit and Polish for Husbands*, 172.

19. This information comes, in part, from AllYouCanRead.com.

20. Taken from http://www.decipher.com/content/pdf/mk03-boycrazy.pdf.

21. Amazon.com, "*Cosmopolitan*; editorial review,"
    http://www.amazon.com.

22. Seen at TeenVoices.com.

Chapter 6

1. National Coalition for the Protection of Children and
   Families, "Internet Pornography,"
   http://nationalcoalition.org/.

2. Sharon Secor, "Especially for Parents, News and
   Commentary by Sharon Secor," April 2003:
   http://www.obscenitycrimes.org/espforparents/
   espforparents2003-04.cfm.

3. National Academies survey cited in The All I Need, "More
   Students Go Online to Get Ahead in School":
   http://www.theallineed.com/computers/internet_
   promise_concern.htm.

4. According to a study by the London School of Economics
   and Political Science:
   http://news.scotsman.com/latest.cfm?id=3235784.

5. Joe Churcher, Joe, Martha Linden, and Pat Hurst, "Talks
   Aim to Tackle Internet Child Porn," The Scotsman.com,
   July, 21, 2004,
   http://news.scotsman.com/latest.cfm?id=3235784.

6. John Carr, Internet adviser, NCH (National Children's
   Homes, London, England), quoted in ,"Parents still under-
   estimate internet risks" (Dr. Margaret Bober, et al),
   http://personal.lse.ac.uk/bober/PressReleaseJuly04.pdf.

7. Keith Dunn in discussion with the author, August 2004.

8. For more information, go to CLASServices.com.

9. GetNetWise.org, "Guide to Internet Terms: A Glossary"
   www.getnetwise.org/glossary.php.

10. Ellen Edwards, *The Washington Post*, Wednesday, May 14,
    2004, C01.

11. *Business Wire,* December 19, 2000.
12. *Journal of the American Medical Association,* 2001 Pew Study, cited in American Family Online, "Statistics": http://www.afo.net/statistics.htm.
13. Ramona Richards, "Dirty Little Secret," *Today's Christian Woman,* September/October 2003, 58–62.
14. Dr. Joel Hunter, senior pastor, Northland, A Church Distributed, in a sermon titled "A Radical Fall/Paradise Lost," delivered during the week of January 25, 2004.
15. Covington and Swindoll, "Pornography: No Longer a Dirty Little Secret," Crosswalk.com: http://www.crosswalk.com/faith/1224639.html.
16. Sean Dunn, *Momentum: Gaining Ground with God* (Grand Rapids, MI: Fleming H. Revell, 2004), 94.
17. Pamela Paul, "The Porn Factor": http://www.time.com/time/2004/sex/article/the_porn_factor_in_the_01a.html.
18. ISP is the acronym for Internet Service Provider (America Online, EarthLink, MSN, CompuServe, etc.).

CHAPTER 7

1. http://www.brainyquote.com/quotes/authors/a/abraham_lincoln.html.
2. DOE, NCES 1999-057; Department of Justice, NCJ 178906, 1999, 63.
3. Reynolds, *Sin City,* p. 104.
4. Stephen James, personal interview, April 2004.
5. Taylor Dockery, "My Commitment to America's Future," *Pulpit Helps,* Vol. 29, No. 4, April 2004.
6. Christine Caine, *A Life Unleashed* (New York: Warner Faith, 2004), 92.

APPENDIX A

1. Stacie Orrico (Sparrow/Virgin recording artist), in an interview by the Associated Press before the MTV Asia Awards (2004) "Orrico decries Spears, Aguilera," http://www.newsabahtimes.com.my/February2004/16.2/leisure1.htm.

APPENDIX C

1. "Take that, rewind it back" are lyrics found within the song.

Web Sources

The Web site addresses (URLs) recommended are solely offered as a resource to the reader. The citation of these Web sites does not in any way imply an endorsement on the part of the authors or the publisher, nor do the authors or publisher vouch for their content for the life of this book. Due to the nature of this book's topic, some sites may be graphic or candid in their content.

INTRODUCTION

http://www.movieguide.org
http://www.nationalcoalition.org
http://www.kidsfirst.org
http://www.commonsensemedia.org
http://www.lionlamb.org
http://www.mediafamily.org
http://www.fcc.gov/parents
http://www.onemillionmoms.com
http://www.onemilliondads.com
http://www.onemillionyouth.com

CHAPTER ONE

http://www.bigeye.com/sexeducation/history.html
http://www.jackinworld.com/library/articles/kinsey.html
http://www.people.virginia.edu/~rjh9u/sexhistory.html
http://www.u.arizona.edu/ic/mcbride/ws200/grp2rrep.thm

CHAPTER TWO

http://www.obscenitycrimes.org

http://www.centex.net/~elliott/1960/html
http://www.alaskajim.com/polls/2002topsongs1970s_results
    .htm
http://www.fact-index.com
http://www.cpyu.org
http://www.mercurynews.com
http://www.media-awareness.ca/
http://www.bahec.org/health%20education/teens.html

CHAPTER THREE

http://www.nationalcoalition.org/
http://www.fiftiesweb.com/tv50htm
http://www.tvland.com
http://www.tvtome.com
http://www.fcc.gov/vchip/
http://www.media-awareness.ca/
http://www.fadetoblack.com
http://www.awesome80s.com
http://www.super70s.com
http://www.truelies.org
http://www.about.com
http://www.imdb.com
http://www.cnn.com
http://www.uweb.ucsb.edu/~katiej/brain.html
http://www.musicsearch.aol.com
http://www.thewb.com
http://www.nytimes.com
http://www.washingtimes.com
http://www.psc.disney.go.com

CHAPTER FOUR

http://www.filmsite.org/20sintro.html
http://imdb.com/

http://www.filmsite.org/30sintro.html
http://weeklywire.com/ww/06-14-99/alibi_facts.html
http://www.aolsvc.worldbook.aol.com/wb/Article?id=ar25
7510
http://www.fact-
index.com/l/li/list_of_hollywood_movie_studios.html
http://www.un-official.com/GWH/GWMain.html
http://www.filmsite.org/oscars.html
http://www.hollywoodteenmovies.com
http://www.thebratpacksite.com/

CHAPTER FIVE

http://www.allyoucanread.com
http://www.amazon.com
http://www.americangirl.com
http://www.forerunner.com/forerunner/X0332_Ted_Bundy.
html

CHAPTER SIX

http://www.nationalcoalition.org/
http://www.time.com/time/2004/sex/article/the_porn_fac
tor_in_the_01a.html
http://www.crosswalk.com/faith/1224639.html
http://www.obscenitycrimes.org/espforparents/
espforparents2003-04.cfm
http://www.obscenitycrimes.org
http://www.chatdanger.com/
http://www.xanga.com
http://kdcop.com

CHAPTER SEVEN

http://www.moralityinmedia.org/

Readers' Guide

*For Personal Reflection
or Group Discussion*

Readers' Guide

It's no secret that our culture is awash in sex-related images and information, and the consequences are impacting our families dramatically. Combine this emphasis on sex with the fact that most teenagers do not believe in moral absolutes, and it's obvious why alarming trends are developing and/or being established. Pornography, for example, is a huge business, and it enters our homes through a wide range of media.

That's probably why you picked up this book. You want to be the best parent you can be, and you realize that part of your "job description" involves keeping communication channels open and understanding the sex-related challenges children (and adults) face.

The following discussion questions will assist you in exploring key themes and issues of this book. Perhaps they'll serve as a "refresher" course for some of you who are quite familiar with sexuality in the media. But others of you, who for various reasons aren't as aware, may be a bit uncomfortable with the subject matter. That's understandable. So much is happening so quickly, and the statistics are alarming.

Wherever you are in your journey as a parent, however, relax. Many parents are trying to figure out how to respond to sexual issues their children face in various media; you are not alone! Sexuality is a challenging topic in and of itself, without even factoring in the many ways in which our children are being exposed to it every day. That's precisely why we all need to learn more and be proactive in helping our children understand what's happening in their culture and learn to make wise, godly choices that have positive consequences.

As you consider the following questions, prayerfully reflect on how they relate to you and your family, as well as other people you know. If one of the questions hits a particularly sensitive "nerve," ask yourself why. When you discover a resource that might help your family, explore it more deeply.

There's a lot at stake for everyone.

A major spiritual battle is taking place concerning sex in the media—a battle for the hearts and minds of our children (and for ours, too). God calls us to train our children well, and these days that involves learning things we never imagined we'd have to learn—at least so soon!

Feel free to adapt these questions to your particular situation. Perhaps you'll think about and/or discuss one or two in great depth, and spend less time on others. That's okay. Life is a journey, and where you are right now will influence which questions especially connect with you and/or the members of your discussion group.

CHAPTER 1

1. What cultural changes have you seen concerning sexuality that didn't exist, or were emphasized far less, when you were growing up?

2. Were you surprised as you read about the historical emphases on sexuality? Why or why not?

3. Why do you think Satan uses sex to separate people from God?

4. Which statistics in this chapter surprised you? Why?

5. According to the author, why is it so important for us to communicate biblical truth concerning the media and its overemphasis on sexuality?

6. We know it is important for us to pray for our children every day. What obstacles (or excuses) hinder us from doing this?

CHAPTER 2

1. What impact is music having on our children today? How do you think sexual themes in music are different now than they were years ago?

2. How can we learn more about the music our children are listening to? How can we foster those learning opportunities in our daily lives?

3. Do you agree that teens gravitate toward the music that "speaks the loudest to their souls"? Why or why not? Feel free to describe a real-life situation, if you are discussing these questions in a group setting.

4. What are some things parents should not do when trying to help their children make godly decisions about music?

5. The author mentioned monitoring music that children download from the Internet. What is involved in doing this?

6. What's the difference between trying to control our children's music, on one hand, and teaching them to evaluate the music they listen to?

7. Why do you think the author emphasizes parental modeling? What are some examples of the "smallest things" we do or say that count?

Chapter 3

1. What impact do you think television is having on your child(ren)? Explain your answer.

2. Clearly it is important for us to spend quantity time with our children. Yet that's often quite difficult. How are you dealing with this challenge?

3. Why do you think sexual content on television has increased so dramatically in recent years?

4. When a child has been watching inappropriate television programs, what are some alternative responses to "inflicting blame and shame" on the child?

5. Which of James Steyer's suggestions did you find most helpful?

6. What's involved in being a "media gatekeeper" for children? Which questions do we need to ask ourselves, and our children, in order to be effective media gatekeepers?

7. How does Galatians 6:7–8 relate to the issues explored in this chapter?

8. What are some positive ways to talk with and educate our children about sexuality portrayed on television?

Chapter 4

1. How should our society apply the First Amendment to sex-related material, especially in movies?

2. Do you think "rating systems" are effective? Why or why not?

3. What trends have you noticed in "teen movies"?

4. How can we better educate ourselves concerning the movies our children watch?

5. How can we help our children learn what they need to know in order to face movie-related issues with godly, biblical perspectives?

6. Why do many parents avoid having conversations with their older children about sexuality in media, including movies? What happens when parents stop "selling" key truths to their children and run away from the challenges of doing so?

7. How important a role do movies play in your family? How can you make movies excellent teaching tools? If you can, share an example from your experience.

CHAPTER 5

1. Why is it important to note that younger children often read "teen" magazines and that teens often read adult magazines?

2. What are some practical ways in which we can help our children separate truth from myth in what they read?

3. How should we respond to the statistics mentioned in this chapter? Which one(s) did you find most interesting (or startling)? Why?

4. The author stressed the importance of studying the magazines our children read. Why is that so important? And what should we do when we discover that many messages found there either are not true or are only partly true?

5. What is involved in "guarding" our hearts? (See Proverbs 4:22–23.)

6. What is lust? Why is it so damaging?

7. Chances are, if your child is at least seven years of age, he or she sees some of the magazines mentioned at the end of this chapter. What are some positive ways in which you can open up meaningful dialogue concerning points raised in this chapter?

CHAPTER 6

1. Why is it important for parents to know at least the basics about computers and Internet use?

2. How can you reduce the risks of your children, or those in your sphere of influence, viewing pornography on the Internet?

3. What is sexual addiction, and why is it so common even among Christians?

4. Discuss some of the basic tips we need to teach our children, including "new friends" on the Internet, not providing personal information, etc.

5. What are some signs that a child is involved in Internet pornography? To whom might you turn if you discover your child is addicted to pornography?

6. Why do you think many Christians are afraid to talk about this issue?

Chapter 7

1. Do you really believe a spiritual battle is happening? Why is this issue often overlooked, disregarded, or overemphasized?

2. What's the difference between being a child's parent and being a child's friend?

3. Reflect on your life for a few moments. In which area(s) are you not being conformed to the image of Christ? What are you willing to do about this wrongdoing?

4. When our children make mistakes, how does God want us to respond? (Hint: God offers us his forgiveness, and so much more.)

5. What are some other ways in which you might open up and/or strengthen the lines of communication between you and your child(ren)?

6. The author mentioned the danger of parents letting their emotions sidetrack them as they talk with their children. Which emotion or emotions tend to derail your communication with your child?

7. Which of the author's "pointers" at the end of this chapter connected with you? Why? Take time to discuss some of them in detail.

The Word at Work Around the World

A vital part of Cook Communications Ministries is our international outreach, Cook Communications Ministries International (CCMI). Your purchase of this book, and of other books and Christian-growth products from Cook, enables CCMI to provide Bibles and Christian literature to people in more than 150 languages in 65 countries.

Cook Communications Ministries is a not-for-profit, self-supporting organization. Revenues from sales of our books, Bible curricula, and other church and home products not only fund our U.S. ministry, but also fund our CCMI ministry around the world. One hundred percent of donations to CCMI go to our international literature programs.

CCMI reaches out internationally in three ways:

· Our premier International Christian Publishing Institute (ICPI) trains leaders from nationally led publishing houses around the world.

· We provide literature for pastors, evangelists, and Christian workers in their national language.

· We reach people at risk—refugees, AIDS victims, street children, and famine victims—with God's Word.

Word Power, God's Power

Faith Kidz, RiverOak, Honor, Life Journey, Victor, NexGen — every time you purchase a book produced by Cook Communications Ministries, you not only meet a vital personal need in your life or in the life of someone you love, but you're also a part of ministering to José in Colombia, Humberto in Chile, Gousa in India, or Lidiane in Brazil. You help make it possible for a pastor in China, a child in Peru, or a mother in West Africa to enjoy a life-changing book. And because you helped, children and adults around the world are learning God's Word and walking in his ways.

Thank you for your partnership in helping to disciple the world. May God bless you with the power of his Word in your life.

For more information about our
international ministries, visit www.ccmi.org.

Additional copies of *SEX, LIES, AND THE MEDIA*
and other Life Journey titles
are available wherever good books are sold.

If you have enjoyed this book,
or if it has had an impact on your life,
we would like to hear from you.

Please contact us at:

LIFE JOURNEY
Cook Communications Ministries, Dept. 201
4050 Lee Vance View
Colorado Springs, CO 80918

Or visit our Web site: www.cookministries.com